Lending Your Leadership

Lending
Your Leadership

How Pastors Are Redefining Their
Role in Community Life

Nelson Granade

THE
ALBAN
INSTITUTE
Herndon, Virginia
www.alban.org

The Alban Institute
2121 Cooperative Way, Suite 100
Herndon, VA 20171

Scripture quotations unless otherwise noted are from the Holy Bible, New International Version, copyright © 1973, 1978, 1984, International Bible Society, and are used by permission of Zondervan Publishing House.

Scripture quotations marked KJV are from the King James Version of the Bible.

Cover design by Mary Byrd Productions.

Library of Congress Cataloging-in-Publication Data

Granade, Nelson.
  Lending your leadership : how pastors are redefining their role in community life / Nelson Granade; foreword by Robert D. Dale.
    p. cm.
  Includes bibliographical references (p.   ).
  ISBN-13: 978-1-56699-310-4
  ISBN-10: 1-56699-310-5
  1. Pastoral theology. 2. Community leadership—Religious aspects—Christianity. I. Title.

  BV4325.G73 2006
  253—dc22
                                    2005036033

11   10   09   08   07   06   VG   1   2   3   4   5   6   7

Contents

Foreword

"Some assembly required." That's the warning on some gifts we receive or items we buy. If the gift or item in question is a jigsaw puzzle, the warning is an understatement! Imagine the circuitous process of assembling a jigsaw puzzle. First, the box is opened and emptied onto a large, flat surface. All of the pieces are turned picture-side up. The picture on the outside of the box becomes the guiding pattern for the puzzle assembler. At this stage, most of us take a deep breath, wonder if we're in over our heads, but still plunge into the process. Commonly, we find the straight pieces—edges and corners—and put them together. Then, we match up the most obvious colors and patterns and begin to shape the picture. We next fill in the more nuanced colors and patterns, the pieces that take time and care to match. Finally, we're left with those last, odd pieces that don't seem to "fit" into this puzzle. Slowly, and sometimes almost magically, we fit them together to complete the final picture. It's a relief when the empty box's picture and the completed puzzle on the table before us both are the same. Suddenly, we see the uneven assembly process was worth it all. We've solved the puzzle.

In like manner, ministers in today's world know how complicated and nuanced leadership has become. We also recognize that faith communities and service communities overlap in complex ways. Finally, we have a resource to solve this ministry puzzle. But, make no mistake, some assembly will still be required.

Community Leadership: Pouring out the Puzzle

Nelson Granade's *Lending Your Leadership: How Pastors Are Redefining Their Role in Community Life* places a pastoral leadership puzzle on the table before us. Granade has provided a process of finding edges and prominent features. Finally, with patience, those more nuanced patterns are mastered and the puzzle meshes into a beautiful mosaic of ministry. Ministry is always a hands-on, learn-as-you-go activity. That's why some assembly is always required.

Many of the challenges in community leadership are beyond the practical reach of seminary training. "Seminary" simply means "seedbed." It's only after the fledgling leader is transplanted into a working field of ministry that one's contribution to community leadership can be fully discovered and crafted.

Pastors and practitioners of Christian ministry aren't surprised by the many facets of contemporary faith that emerge for leaders. After all, in the practice of ministry, we wrestle with complicated relationships, complex organizations, and difficult issues. But, as Granade skillfully shows, ministry leaders have unique contributions to make.

Jesus modeled a pattern of ministry and leadership for us. Strategically, he anchored himself in the middle of his community but ministered on its margins. Middle and margins—they are the primary puzzle pieces.

Just like solving a jigsaw puzzle, the big patterns and the edges are the keys in leadership. Jesus gave himself to the kingdom of God. That was his center, the middle of his ministry. But he risked leadership on the edges of life, culture, and community. That's where life is most dynamic and where systems are most apt to stretch and change. We can, and we must, take the middles and the margins seriously too if we are to solve ministry's puzzles.

Mooring in the Middle: Sorting the Puzzle

Lending Your Leadership centers itself wisely in pastoral identity, calling, self-awareness, vision, ministry gifts, and faith's values. Granade masterfully weaves biblical stories, historical lessons, and common sense into a tapestry for leadership. This tapestry stakes out the middle for leaders and provides a place to announce, "Here I stand." While the middle is a frequent theme in leadership, it sometimes is lost or compromised in the actual tug-of-war called community ministry. The middle is both the starting line and the finish line for community. We begin in the middle and return to it as well. Our spiritual center in the kingdom of God moors ministry puzzles and brings us home.

Ministry on the Margins: Solving the Puzzle

The edges are the most productive places where minister-leaders practice community leadership. What are some margins that both guide and challenge us in ministry?

- The directional margin: the "face" of leadership. Christian ministry turns faith inside out, pioneers new paradigms, and revises directions for faith. Ministry, when based on the nature of Christian mission, reaches beyond itself. Yet, it's tempting in ministry to make "my" church into "my sanctuary," my place of retreat. In that case, we turn our backs on the world and focus our energies on the internal, pulpit-and-pew environment.

- The connectional margin: "holding hands" in leadership. Christian ministry turns faith toward the far side. Ministry, based on John 3:16's "for God so loved the world," bridges contexts, mindsets, and eras for Christ. Moving between arenas beyond the local congregation spans issues and audiences. This is where connections are made and new communities are established.

- The transformational margin: making the old new in leadership. Christian leaders have a history of turning communities of ministry upside down. Ministry, when based on the nature of God, shifts paradigms and reverses definitions of faith. The book of Acts reminds us that God's kingdom makes faith and life topsy-turvy (Acts 17:6). Some would argue that healthy faith actually rights and transforms a needy world.

Lending Leadership: No Operator's Manual

When minister-leaders catch a vision of ministry across the full reach and range of their communities, we, as Luther once described the risks of courageous ministry, "sin boldly." While there's no operator's manual for community leadership, *Lending Your Leadership* fills a gap in pastoral literature and helps us solve the ministry puzzle. Be ready, though. Some assembly is required.

Robert D. Dale
Ray and Ann Spence Network for
Congregational Leadership

Preface

One of the mysteries of the Christian's faith journey is how it can be both serendipitous and providential. I have no doubt in God's ability to accomplish God's will in our lives, our congregations, and our communities. How God gets us there, however, is always an adventure. Community leadership is not something I set out to do. In fact, I rather fell into it by what seemed like chance but, I believe, turned out to be providence. I offer my experience in community leadership not as the account of an expert but as the story of one pastor who has discovered God's calling and movement outside a traditional congregational structure. It is my hope that in hearing my story you will find something of benefit for your story. It is my trust that God will bring us all into God's ultimate will. Enjoy the adventure!

I'd like to thank my congregation, the First Baptist Church of North Wilkesboro, North Carolina, for graciously lending the time and attention of their pastor to many community ventures and to the efforts of this book. I'd also like to thank the people of Wilkes County, North Carolina, for welcoming a pastor into what might seem to some to be unusual circles. I am grateful to the members of the Wilkes County lectionary study group, my fellow community activist/minister Paul

Hugger, and my friend Larry Gregg for their continued help in support of both my ministry and this book. Special thanks to my editor, Beth Ann Gaede, for wise suggestions and patience, both of which made this a better book. Most of all, I'd like to thank my family—my wife Sharilyn and my children James Douglas and Emily—for their encouragement and support as I've sought to stretch my leadership beyond typical pastoral expectations.

This book is dedicated to my father, Napp Granade, and in appreciation to my mother, Sarah Granade, who instilled with their example a desire to help bridge the gap between our congregations and our communities.

Chapter 1

A Pastoral Response

The Crisis of Community Leadership

"You look at things differently from anyone else here." People have made that comment to me on more than one occasion when I have attended community meetings. It took me a while to figure out that this was a compliment, one that affirms something I should have known already—that pastors have a calling and training different from that of anyone else in community meetings. When pastors are not present among community leaders, pastoral questions go unasked and unanswered.

Most pastors realize that there is more power in a good question than in a quick answer. We are trained, through pastoral care and counseling classes and practice, to ask the right questions. Just as a good question can open a counselee to a whole new way of thinking, so a powerful question can open a community group to a whole new way of acting. Sometimes changes in community groups happen when one well-placed question provides a tipping point. Even more powerful, however, are the changes brought about when, over time, a pastor earns both the trust and the right to ask the hard questions.

Most pastors understand that there are spiritual dimensions to every problem—including community issues. As pastoral counselor Howard Clinebell puts it, "Though often not so obvious and in some cases completely hidden, there is an existential-

1

spiritual dimension in every problem with which pastor and parishioner struggle in counseling."[1] This same "existential-spiritual dimension" exists within the wider arena of community change. As Clinebell further states:

> People need sound values and meanings to be healthy. Growth toward Spirit-centered wholeness must include growth in life-giving values and ethical commitments. The epidemic of moral confusion and value distortions in our society is the seedbed within which are bred many of the psychological, psychosomatic, interpersonal, and spiritual problems that bring people to counseling and therapy. The widespread collapse of old authority-centered and institutionally-validated value systems has left millions of people feeling as though they are drifting in mid-ocean in a small boat without a rudder, a compass, or a chart during a storm. . . . Often they are unaware of the ethical roots of their pain.[2]

As community leaders seek to sort through the continual changes facing our society, few will have an awareness of the underlying spiritual-ethical dimensions or possess the skills with which to address the cracks in unseen foundations. A pastor, however, has skills he or she can use to make a difference. The same pastoral-care skills she or he uses to help an individual or family become aware of and address underlying spiritual-ethical issues can be used to help a community group identify and address even larger ethical concerns. For instance, though it seems unwise to turn a meeting about a proposed roadway into a counseling session, a pastor can help facilitate the deep feelings often stirred by signs of change. By actively helping people listen to one another, we might be able to mediate discussions (even when we are not chairing the meeting) and avoid the breaking of community that often results from hotly disputed decisions. By raising questions about how people are affected by the road construction, or by new traffic patterns and route changes, we are practicing Christian ethics. We help the entire group consider the impact the proposed changes might entail, whether they be negative (displacing lower-income housing or disrupting fragile ecosystems) or positive (creating safer traffic patterns or spurring economic development that accompanies good highways). Not all community leaders are unaware of underlying ethical issues, but a pastor's presence adds an extra spotlight on such concerns.

An example of how one well-placed pastoral question can make a difference to an entire community can be seen in an educational impasse within my own community. One of my earliest forays into community leadership involved a school-bond referendum. Unfortunately, our group, which was concerned with building new schools to advance education, got an education in politics when a strange compilation of parties united to defeat the school bond initiative. Our group, though discouraged, was not deterred. A new plan was formed, and a joint meeting was set for the county commissioners to hear the school board's new proposal. When no action was taken at the joint board meeting, my friend, the former rector of Saint Paul's Episcopal Church in Wilkesboro, North Carolina, Ken Asel and I decided to attend the next meeting of the county commissioners. We wanted to see how the commissioners would respond to the school board's new proposal.

It soon became apparent, however, that they planned to do nothing about the proposal—except to delay a decision until after the next election. We sat through a two-hour meeting (during which schools were not discussed) and then through another hour of closed session (for which the commissioners

3

disappeared into a back room). Everyone else in the room (including the reporters) left during the closed session—as usual attenders, they knew that the only business left was for the commissioners to return to open session to adjourn.

Despite what seemed like wasted time and effort, Ken and I were determined to see progress, so like Horton the Elephant we sat and we sat and we sat. If nothing else, we wanted to let the commissioners know that we were not going away. When they returned, the chairman made the mistake of looking my way, and I stood to ask for a point of personal privilege. Before he could say no, I explained that we were interested in the commissioners addressing the school board's proposal. Ken, who at this point was calmer than I, rose beside me and gently raised a simple question. With strength of conviction, he quietly asked, "What about the children of our county? Are you going to address their needs by responding to the school board's proposal tonight?" Silence ensued for what seemed like an hour, and then one commissioner responded: "I think we ought to talk about this issue. It sounds like the people are interested in an answer." They met for another hour, during which time, surprisingly, we were asked for our ideas on how to get the community to support higher taxes for school construction. The discussion produced a process for moving forward with a series of listening sessions throughout the county. Though I'm sure some of the commissioners thought the sessions would produce an outcry against taxes and an excuse to delay school construction, our citizens got behind the new plan. The process culminated in the commissioners voting to fund four new middle schools.

Asking the right pastoral question in the right place at the right time did more than make a difference in the quality of education within our community. It also helped to restore and redefine pastoral leadership within our community. I'll never forget the comment of the sheriff that evening (he was required to attend every commissioners meeting from beginning to end). As we walked out that night, he said, "I've never seen them react like that to anyone. What kind of power do you guys have?" My quick answer to him was "None that I know of."

His question, however, started me pondering the power of pastoral influence within a community. Ken and I had discovered the effectiveness of the pastoral skill of questioning as one way to be a prophetic voice in our community. It felt great to make a difference. I began to wonder: What other ways exist for a pastor to exercise leadership so as to make a difference in his or her community? Was it time to move beyond the valuable but limited area of social ministries? Could the role pastors play locally be strengthened and expanded? Is it possible for pastors to exercise their unique gifts beyond their congregations by joining the wider circle of community leaders? My search to answer these questions has led me into an exciting odyssey that has stretched my concept of pastoral ministry while strengthening my leadership skills.

The Paradox of Community Leadership

We live in a time when people cry for leadership while rejecting leaders. Systems theorist Rabbi Edwin Friedman aptly defined this situation as a state of "leadership toxicity." Others have spoken of a "paradox of leadership." Communities desperately need leaders to guide the way through the challenges of change, but they often reject leaders because of the anxiety associated with such change. Anxious communities, like anxious congregations, can become unhealthy systems and develop unrealistic expectations of leaders. Just as anxious congregations "overfocus on their clergy" and "find it immensely difficult to see the rest of the system,"[3] anxious communities overfocus on community leaders and fail to see the core causes of their apprehension. The community's "blurred vision" generates unrealistic expectations of leaders and distorted ideas about community problems. The leader becomes a magnet for criticism while the community stumbles along failing to see or to address radical economic and cultural shifts. Foundational issues receive little attention and thus continue to be unresolved, creating even higher levels of anxiety. The unfortunate result is that leadership is devalued and those brave enough to offer leadership often decide that the results are not worth the cost.

This paradox of leadership affects all leaders, but it is magnified in traditional leadership roles (public officeholders, civic-group officers, physicians, corporate leaders, clergy, and the like) that carry the baggage of long-standing expectations. Where other leaders are expected to offer creative solutions to dilemmas, traditional leaders are limited by the expectations associated with their roles. Traditional community leaders are faced with a plethora of problems, but they often lack the resources and support to make a true impact. If they step outside their "roles," they risk alienating their shrinking but vital base of support. At the same time, substantial shifts in community life (economic challenges, racial makeup, generational differences, decline of religious bodies, the impact of postmodernism) call for creative solutions to new challenges. In trying to find relevant solutions to contemporary problems, other traditional community leaders face a challenge with which we pastors are all too familiar. How does one creatively engage a new culture without alienating those who would like to maintain the old culture?

I once heard well-known homiletics professor Tom Long give a lecture on "questions we should ask of our preaching."

Long suggested a number of questions that, if pondered, could improve our communication to our congregation. In trying to apply this lesson, I have found that two of these questions are often in conflict with one another—"So what?" and "Does it meet the ritualistic expectation of a sermon?" The "so what" question is one of relevance and demands creativity. In an attempt at relevance, many preachers have added PowerPoint presentations, video clips, art displays, short skits, and a variety of other new techniques to their sermons. Unfortunately these novel approaches often run counter to the question of "ritualistic expectation," making traditional congregations squirm.

Like preachers, other traditional leaders are caught in this same quandary of needing the support of those who have certain expectations of how they are to act and the need to react innovatively to a set of circumstances of which their supporters may not even be aware. Politicians are still expected to make "stump speeches" while being Internet savvy. Business people are expected to give personal service, while selling to a global market. Civic-club leaders are expected to lead their members altruistically to give large amounts of time to special projects in a world in which time has become the currency of the day. And physicians are to be wise dispensers of a broad range of knowledge in a radically changing medical system that requires specialization.

Further complicating this matter of "traditional role expectations" is the pressure to perform (or perhaps to perform miracles). Though community members may not be aware of all the underlying issues, many intuitively feel the stresses upon their community and look for their leadership to "do something!" It reminds me of my ill-fated attempt to coach high school tennis. My only qualification was that I owned a tennis racquet and held a valid chauffeur's license (that is, they really needed somebody to drive the bus). I soon discovered that I was in over my head when I tried to dispense advice to players more skilled than I. One young man seemed to be dragging, so I yelled, "Let's move out there." To which he responded, "Which way?" I suddenly realized that he was expecting some useful information about his court position and that I had no clue as to whether he should move up, back, right, or left. So too, our communities expect results, while neither they nor their leaders have a clue as to which way to move. This need to "do something" can lead to doing the wrong thing or just doing the same thing harder.

Friedman notes that because we lack the abilities to deal with increasing societal stress, our culture has an increasing amount of "free-floating anxiety." This anxiety is further amplified by the abundance of media outlets (the Internet, 24-hour news channels, talk radio, and sensationalist journals) until the mix produces what Friedman terms "leadership toxicity." In other words, the very stress of needing to "find solutions" makes finding solutions almost impossible. This catch-22 plays itself out in our communities when politicians, who are subject to the whims of the voters, are forced to choose between exercising real leadership (doing what is right for the long term), and producing a quick fix. Though we might join with others in labeling this situation "politics as usual," I have found that many of these men and women truly care for their communities and are struggling with the same difficulties as other community leaders. Unfortunately, many who attempt to exercise genuine leadership fall prey to leadership toxicity.

The Loss Of Community Leaders

Given this state of increased demands upon leaders and decreased support of leaders, it is no wonder that our communities are experiencing a loss of leadership. This situation of high demands on leadership, however, is not the only contributing factor to the decreased pool of community leaders. The combination of numerous workforce reductions and an emphasis on globalization has led corporations to place less value on community involvement. Although companies still tout their "pet programs," workers are rarely encouraged to give large amounts of corporate-sponsored volunteer time.

In the community I serve, this trend of declining corporate involvement runs counter to the historical expectation that businesses would provide both leaders and resources to the community. Larger employers continue to show support, but it is no longer a given that they will participate in meeting every community need. Previously, numerous community groups dined at the benevolence trough. Businesses bought new high school band uniforms, "loaned" their executives to the United Way, lent expertise to study committees, provided conference rooms for meetings, and supplied many other resources when asked. Unfortunately, many of these companies are suffering economic difficulty themselves and are no longer able to contribute at high levels. Other companies have grown and shifted their focus from providing community capital to producing stockholder profit. Even companies that are increasing the numbers of employees are less likely now than they were a decade ago to share the leadership skills of their well-educated and financially able workforce with local community organizations.

The reality of the global economy is having a huge impact on local economies—and on the leadership pool. Even rural areas, like the one where I serve as pastor, have felt dynamic shifts in their economies. For some, globalization has meant greater wealth as they have received increased access to less costly imported goods. For others, globalization has created negative effects for which they were ill prepared. Over the past 10 years, our community has experienced the exportation of thousands of blue-collar jobs, leading to the demise of our local textile industry. Although these workers are valiantly trying to retrain for other jobs, most do not have the resources to weather the transition. Thus, community needs are rising while the level of community resources and the number of community leaders are declining.

Amid this crisis, one might expect businesses and industries that are less affected by globalization and more dependent on the strength of the local economy to fill the leadership void—if only for their own benefit. Quite the contrary is happening. As these companies feel the squeeze of economic difficulties beyond their control and the push for higher productivity, they too are forced to cut back on community participation. Even those who continue to encourage local participation no longer have the human resources or local budgets to do so at previous levels. For instance, our power company, which has long been a tremendous local benefactor, has over the past 30 years progressively increased the responsibilities of its district executives (whose job descriptions specify that they represent the company in area communities). Whereas these people used to service one or two counties, they are now spread over three to five.

Ten years ago our district executive was present in our town three or four times a week and was able to serve on numerous local committees. Now he must limit his visits to once or twice a week and be extremely selective about his committee participation. He notes that technology helps him stay in touch and that his company continues to value local involvement, but he expresses disappointment over having insufficient time to be engaged on a more personal level. Likewise, many banks (which have traditionally supplied both funding and volunteers for community events) have replaced local branch executives with regional officers. This move from local to regional to national, and even to global organizational structures, results in fewer people with less time, stretched over larger areas and relating to a greater number of communities. A lessening of involvement in the communities where these companies are located, or that they serve, is the natural if unintended result of these stretched resources.

This pullback of local involvement by businesses and industries to accommodate changing corporate climates results in other community leaders having fewer resources with which to deal with growing problems. For instance, local politicians, who in the past might have been able to influence area industries to donate resources, have less sway with companies focused on global issues. In fact, governing bodies now find themselves "paying" to recruit industries through incentive packages that can include reduced or deferred property taxes, subsidization of relocation expenses, expansion of local utilities, and grants of land or facilities. Meanwhile, voters pressure these political leaders to create jobs while reducing taxes and threaten to vote them out of office if they do not produce. When I encourage strong congregational leaders to consider providing political leadership to our community, their stunned reply is, "Why should I?" They know that the personal demands on public leaders are high, while the odds of making substantial changes are low. They might be willing to work behind the scenes, but they don't care to be in the line of fire.

Effects of Declining
Social Capital on Communities

Given this "local leadership crisis," one might expect civic organizations, charities, and other nonprofit organizations that have community betterment as part of their mission to fill the gap. Though these men and women strive to make a difference, the reality is that their numbers are shrinking and their organizations are graying. These traditional contributors of what has been termed "social capital" are genuinely altruistic and deeply concerned about their communities. Unfortunately their care and concern cannot create the vast resources needed to address ever-growing community needs.

As Robert D. Putnam points out in his article "The Strange Disappearance of Civic America," "Membership records of such diverse organizations as the PTA, the Elks Club, the League of Women Voters, the Red Cross, labor unions, and even bowling leagues show that participation in many conventional voluntary associations has declined by roughly 25 percent to 50 percent over the last two to three decades."[4] Putnam blames television as the main culprit for the decline in social capital. He observes that "most forms of social and media participation are positively correlated" while "television is . . . the only leisure activity that seems to inhibit participation outside the home."[5] Other researchers point to a vast array of issues affecting the decline of social capital, including:

- economic forces;
- sociocultural concerns (crime rates, child poverty, etc.);
- political fallout (scandals, corruptions, careerism among elected officials);
- increased mobility leading to decreased community connection (the average American moves six times in his or her adult life);
- less discretionary time;
- more dual-career families;
- more single mothers;
- individuals taking a longer time to complete education.[6]

The national decline of social capital plays out locally. The predicament of civic organizations, which gallantly try to meet growing community needs with shrinking resources, can certainly be seen in my community. When I moved to Wilkes County, North Carolina, 10 years ago, I visited several civic clubs and felt a real angst in these groups. Each civic club approached me with the pitch often employed by congregations as well—"Please join, because we really need some young blood to carry on our work." Unfortunately, this pitch speaks more to the anxiety of the organization than it does to the desire and gifts of the prospective member.

Whether or not these organizations (or our congregations) are cognizant of it, such statements reflect a change in emphasis from mission to institutional survival. That new emphasis is not inviting to a new generation and will not be heeded by those whom we wish to attract to our clubs or congregations. This situation, however, is not a reflection on the value of these groups. Civic clubs continue to provide valuable service for the betterment of their communities. I sincerely admire these groups and see them do wonderful work within our community. But there are just too few of them dealing with too many issues. Unless there is a rebirth of these organizations, which would require adaptation to generational differences, the level of leadership they can provide will trail off with the decline in their membership.

The Declining Social Capital of Congregations

While we hope that our congregations are more than community clubs, the parallels we see between civic groups and faith communities are frightening. Pastors can certainly relate to the anxieties of civic-club officers who see their organizations declining and graying. Many of us see the same dynamic in our pews and are worried that sociology of religion professors Wade Clark Roof and William McKinney may be right when they project that "the churches of the Protestant establishment, long in a state of decline, will continue to lose ground in numbers and in social power and influence."[7]

Such a statement raises our anxiety and tempts us down the same roads taken by other community leaders. Like the business leader, we are tempted to focus our limited resources on our own "organization" (congregation) or look for help from our "larger corporate entity" (denomination). Like the political leader, we are tempted to withdraw from leadership opportunities—concluding that we can make little public difference at too great a personal cost. Or like the civic-organization or charity leader, we are tempted to narrow our focus and to use our limited resources in maintaining our most valued services for as long as possible. But before we throw up our hands in despair, or blame others for the lack of leadership amid complicated community issues, we pastors must ask ourselves, "What leadership are we willing to lend to help fill the void of a community's capital?"

Dangers of Providing "Nonchurch" Leadership

Though we might like to provide positive leadership to our communities, many factors make it difficult for pastors to do so. Like other local community leaders, pastors are caught in the paradox of leadership. We know all too well the dangers of entering into anxious systems. Many of us have been caught in the crossfire created by attempting to help families find solutions to deep-seated problems. We know that helping stressed systems, whether families, congregations, or communities, can be both a difficult and a dangerous task. Although we are expected to help stressed families and to seek the welfare of our congregation, community leadership is not always a high expectation among members. So why should we add the community's stress to our already demanding ministries? We have enough anxiety of our own as we struggle to bring traditional congregations into a nontraditional world. It is easier to focus solely on our own congregations. After all, they pay our salaries and have a right to expect that we will give them the best of our abilities, attention, and passion.

For some churchgoers, the congregation is their "sanctuary" from the world, and they do not want the pastor bringing in external tensions. Getting involved in community issues can be seen as political, and many want their pastors to be "above politics." Anyone who becomes involved with community leadership will occasionally wade into turbulent waters, and congregations (like all systems) do not want their pastor (leader) making waves. They rather like the incident of Jesus calming the storm and would like their pastor to perform the same miracle in their own fretful lives. Pastors who choose to make waves might be put on the next boat out of town! Thus pastors share the same private risk assumed by any public leader. We might wish to lead—but at what cost?

Obstacles for Pastors Providing Community Leadership

Even if we choose to offer leadership, the traditional platforms from which we might lead are no longer stable. We are no longer granted instant respect or a place of influence by virtue of our position. Like other traditional leaders, we have seen our influence in the community dwindle. Whether we like it or not, our level of influence has traditionally been related to the size of our congregations. In the eyes of some, our authority flows from our ability to influence a large number of people. Thus numerical decline in many congregations results in a decline in community influence. Accompanying these shifts within congregational life are dramatic shifts within culture. As culture tends to change faster than our congregations and ministry styles, our relevance and right to speak can be called into question. In many communities the pastor's role has gone from trusted advisor to designated prayer-giver at park dedications—if he or she is even invited to play that part.

Even in rural areas, where a pastor's traditional roles are more likely still to be honored, there is more emphasis on ceremony than substance. When my friend Ben Trawick served as pastor of a rural Presbyterian congregation in Virginia, it fell to him to "bless" the annual horse show. "What kind of blessing do you give to a horse show?" he asked. The answer was as succinct as they wished him to be—"a very short one!" In other words, it was made clear that his role was a perfunctory one and that the people were there to see horses, not to listen to prayers.

Pastors who still perform wedding ceremonies for couples not affiliated with the congregation often encounter this same feeling that they serve as window dressing. Such couples have little relationship to the congregation or pastor and show little interest in developing such a relationship. I once thought that these might be outreach opportunities, but have found through dozens of weddings that most couples (unless they have a prior faith commitment) want little more from the church than a token blessing and the required signature on a legal document. They don't care about why we will not allow the bride's cousin or best friend to sing pop or country music selections in a wedding ceremony. After all, they are "renting" the facilities and often think they are "renting" the pastor as well. When our rites carry little theological or ecclesiological meaning to the participants, then our ability to influence their spiritual growth is greatly diminished. This condition, which can be easily seen around weddings, is reflected in every public arena of ministry.

Pastoral Responsibility for Declining Influence

We cannot, however, blame our lack of influence totally upon our congregations or communities. When local pastors fail to be involved in their communities, even if they think their reasons for doing so are sound, community residents begin to view all pastors as nostalgic relics whose job is simply to remind people to "be good." When television evangelists issue blanket condemnations on sensitive moral dilemmas without offering positive alternatives, all clergy pay the price of being considered irrelevant and judgmental. When well-meaning but untrained preachers speak in trite idioms that fail to show an understanding of the intricacies of complicated community dynamics, all who attempt to translate an ancient faith to a contemporary world come off sounding like buffoons. And when denominations fail to supervise the clergy in their charge adequately, we all pay for the sins of the few by losing the respect of many.

In each of these cases clergy get stereotyped, a tendency that plays to clichéd community caricatures of clergy. Whether these generalized notions of clergy are positive (such as the kindly old pastor) or negative (such as predator clergy), they represent an unrealistic picture of a diverse group of people with varying gifts, serving through distinctive traditions. Although these characterizations (like all generalizations) are both

17

unfair and untrue, their unfortunate result, if they go unchallenged, is the same. Characterizations, in any form, tend to strip those stereotypically labeled of their personhood. When we pastors become caricatures instead of flesh-and-blood people, our ability to share in meaningful relationships is stripped away. Without the ability to relate to individuals, we cannot begin to relate to our communities, and we lose our opportunities to influence and lead.

Given these spurious stereotypes of clergy, it is no wonder that we have moved from the top of the Gallup organization's "Honesty and Ethics of Professions" poll when it was first taken in the late 1970s down to the upper-mid-range in the latest available poll (Nov. 14-16, 2003). Pastors trail behind nurses, medical doctors, veterinarians, pharmacists, dentists, college teachers, engineers, and policemen. The good news is that we have recovered somewhat from the Catholic sexual abuse scandals of 2002 (when the percentage of clergy rated ethically as "very high" or "high" by respondents dropped from 64 percent to 52 percent). The 2003 poll shows that 56 percent of respondents rated clergy "very high" or "high" in ethical standards. The bad news is that we are still well below the ratings of clergy from the 1970s and 1980s, when 60 percent to 67 percent of respondents identified us as having "high" or "very high" ethical standing.[8]

The most disturbing news, however, out of the 2003 poll is that younger people are much more critical of clergy. Only 44 percent of 18-to-29-year-olds consider clergy to have "high" or "very high" honesty and ethical standards (compared to 65 percent of those of age 65 and older).[9] This group's negative perception of clergy might result from a number of situations (negative personal encounters with clergy, negative public perceptions of clergy, or the lack of positive pastoral models to

counteract negative perceptions). Which is worse, however—
that young people have negative perceptions of clergy, or that
they are not engaged in our congregations and therefore don't
know us? Ironically, this finding puts the pastor in the place of
hoping that our low ranking is not derived from negative encounters with clergy but from the lack of encounters with any
clergy at all. Either way, the result is the same—we are losing
our standing and trust with younger generations, and it becomes our responsibility to engage them where they are: in our
communities.

A Challenge Worth Accepting

Given that pastors not only suffer from the decline of influence
facing all traditional leaders (especially among rising generations), but also face the challenges of congregations in transition demanding more time and attention, one wonders whether
a pastor can truly provide community leadership. Clerical col-
lars, stoles, or dark suits no longer provide us instant respect
and leadership opportunity with any age group or in any community. We are hesitant to add to our workload, busy sched-
ules, and stress levels to step toward that from which others are
stepping away. Even if a pastor is willing to take on this added
responsibility, how can that pastor find leadership roles in systems where pastors are no longer routinely granted places of
involvement? The questions associated with the "if and can" of
local leadership will be addressed in chapter 2. The questions
of "why and should" of public pastoral investment will be discussed in chapter 3. And the questions of "when and how" of
local involvement will be the topic in chapter 4. Once these
questions are addressed, we will seek ways to expand our model
of "lending our leadership" and to explore the benefits that

this model will provide to our communities, our congregations, and our personal ministries.

As daunting as this task may seem, it may offer many rewards. As one consultant humorously put it when addressing our local hospital board, "We have a wealth of basic improvement opportunities." The situation may seem discouraging, but it also gives new opportunity for redefining our role in more helpful ways to our community and congregation. We have the chance to move past limiting stereotypes, which never contained as much power as we might have presumed, to new modes of personal engagement that offer us opportunities to gain greater credibility in all of our ministries. If we are to restore and redefine the leadership role of the pastor in community, we will have to earn the right to do so.

The good news is that earned leadership is always more powerful than positional leadership. In fact, as local pastors engage our communities and earn the right to lead, the role of pastor will be strengthened. Negative examples from clergy affect us all, but so do positive ones. More important, of all community leaders, we clergy are the only ones who bring with our calling the rich resources of faith.

As many of our communities suffer through dramatic transitions, they need people who are able to see more than what appears on the surface, leaders who can bring a sense of hope and vision. As frustrations raise the level of conflict and partisanship, our fellow citizens need people who can speak words of peace and point to paths of cooperation. As other leaders pull back amid the pressures of a challenging culture, our neighbors need a demonstration of our solid investment of time and talent as much as the people of Israel needed the symbol of Jeremiah's investment in a parcel of land amid the fall of Jerusalem. And as people in our towns turn in one direction and then another for answers to the complicated questions of life to-gether, they need leaders who value truth over expediency. As the bearers of the hope of the gospel, we can keep faith in and with our congregations and communities. It is my firm belief that both need our leadership now more than ever.

Chapter 2
Squirrels in The Road
Adapting to New Opportunities

"Every time I turned, the dumb squirrel darted the same way. I couldn't help but hit the poor thing," said an upset parishioner. Anyone who has driven for long has probably had the same experience. Squirrels just don't know how to react to cars. They do not fare well in encounters with this strange and powerful predator, the automobile. Squirrels are not stupid. These resourceful creatures have been around for ages. But with the invention of the automobile and the expansion of roadways, squirrels came upon a brand-new threat. Darting back and forth works well for evading a hawk, but just getting out of the way quickly might be a better tactic for surviving an encounter with a car going 45 miles an hour. Perhaps squirrels will one day adapt, but given the evidence along the road, it may take a while.

When facing the challenges of postmodernism, a pastor trained for modernity can sometimes feel like a squirrel trying to dodge an approaching tractor-trailer.[1] We dart to and fro using the skills we learned in seminary, conferences, and personal experience, but we have never seen anything like this era, and we don't know quite what to do. As author Jim Kitchens notes, "Our best efforts at ministry seem to be about a half-beat behind some new pulse that is beginning to course through the culture."[2] No matter how hard we try, or encourage our congregations to try, we cannot breathe life into our old methodologies. Most of them simply do not work any more. We begin to wonder if we can provide effective leadership to our congregations, much less our communities.

Pastors and congregations are not the only ones that feel like squirrels in the road. Many of our communities are facing radical cultural, demographic, and economic shifts. Congregations and local communities that do not adapt to changing "threats" risk meeting the same fate as those squirrels along the roadside. Even though much material has been produced to help congregations understand and adapt to postmodernism, this literature reads to a modern like a foreign language. A baby boomer scanning a book on postmodernism can feel utterly lost searching for "data and solutions" (terms of modernity's scientific rationalism), only to find "hints, clues, and approaches" (postmodernism's subjective terms of relativity).

I must admit that the first time I heard the term "postmodern" it sounded a bit oxymoronic to me. Taking the term literally (like a good modern), I wondered, "how can something be 'beyond contemporary?'" As pastor and author Brian McLaren explains in *The Church on the Other Side*, "Postmodernism is a rather bizarre term at first glance, a kind of absurdity rather like 'pre-ancientism.' However, its very oddness seems to be a good reason to keep it for now, because the concepts of postmodernism do seem odd, at least from the outsider's perspective."[3] The very term "postmodernism" is intended to challenge us moderns to move beyond our comfort zones of rationalism and certainty into less comfortable areas of relativism and ambiguity. Like it or not, the challenges of postmodernism will begin to make postmoderns of us all as an emerging future strips away the façade of certainty from a passing time and exposes the foundational cracks in our "irrational reliance on rationalism." Thus the term "postmodernism," which at first sounds like an odd way of describing a strange time, is now an apt means of identifying an emerging era that, by its nature, rejects the rigidity of definitions.

The Acceleration of Change

Even when we begin to get a sense of what postmodernism means for ministry, it remains difficult for pastors and congregations to keep up with the accelerated pace of change in today's culture. It isn't as if we have to dodge one lone vehicle on a backcountry road; we are caught on the interstate, where hundreds of cars and trucks whiz by at 70 miles an hour. Pastors wonder: can we provide leadership in a time that produces a new challenge before we can catch our breath from the last one? Just when we seem to be finding some clues about postmodernism, scholars are beginning to speak of a new "critical postmodernism."[4] Is there now more than one postmodernism, or are we moving into "post-postmodernism?" As leaders of a generation that has experienced the passing of modernity and the dawning of postmodernity, we feel like squirrels given the task of surviving and thriving in a new environment while teaching the other squirrels to do the same.

In a day of transformation, we struggle both with the task of leading people through constant transition and with the impact these transitions make upon the way we lead. Transition requires us to serve as interpreters and teachers while learning a new language. Change necessitates saying good-bye to methods of modernity that no longer work (a grief experience we share as we minister to others who grieve), so that we can say hello to a new day. Effectiveness in a new day requires methods of ministry more relevant to our times. Maintaining a foundation during the transition, however, requires nursing the old systems along until the new practices are strong enough to carry forth a congregation's mission. Amid change, it becomes obvious that to help our congregations and communities make the transition to postmodern life will require retooling our own leadership skills.

But while we may feel like squirrels, we are not. We have more resources than instinctive behavior. We possess intellect, emotion, imagination, and faith. Squirrels, if they could grasp higher concepts, might wish they could get out of the road and into one of these new cars. We, however, are on the road, albeit in old vehicles that cannot keep up with traffic. Even if we take a new vehicle out for a test drive, the newness makes us ill at ease. We can't find the controls; we don't know what the new instruments are for; we can't decipher the owner's manual. To complicate matters, we are on unfamiliar roads, trying to navigate from a confusing map. We attempt to travel the old roads, only to find that they have been closed; we head down new roads to discover that they are still under construction. We know that this new vehicle has innovative features that might make for a smoother journey if we could only figure out the controls and get a feel for our new wheels. We sense that exciting destinations lie before us, but first we must find a more complete map. Or perhaps we might swallow our pride, admit that we are lost, and stop to ask for directions.

Which Direction?

In this journey through postmodernism, we don't know what to expect, but in most areas of life, we are certain that "what was" is no longer—including the traditional role of pastor in community. Roles and expectations of ministers have changed, but what they will become is under negotiation. Perhaps the pastor will become a spirituality specialist, providing "spiritual guidance" for a fee upon referral. Perhaps corporations will seize upon our value as human-relations experts and hire us to be industrial chaplains. Perhaps pastors will become caretakers of ancient truths, serving as curators in religious museums where one can view the relics of a bygone day. Or pastors may find new ways to reengage our communities and culture so as to transform our congregations to minister in a new day. No one knows for sure what is to come, but multiple models and methods of ministry most likely will emerge.

Amid change upon change, it is tempting to keep doing the same thing in the same way, creating familiar respites from the challenge of transition. It is harder to look toward the future, discern what will be required, and adopt yet another new idea. Hesitance to embrace change is especially strong for congregations—they tend to value heritage and tradition more than change and adaptation. It is easy to chastise our congregants as the "frozen chosen," but we pastors too have difficulty accepting newness. We rather like receiving pats on the back for our traditional sermons. We enjoy being sought out for our wise counsel. And we appreciate the work of those who went before us, leaving an inheritance of beautiful sanctuaries and nicely furnished offices. If we are honest, we must admit that our situation can be quite comfortable and that we too are content in our traditional congregations with their accustomed respect for clergy.

But attempting to stop change by refusing to change ourselves will not bring the world back to being the place we might wish it to be. It will, however, create a larger gap between our congregations and a world in transition. The resulting disconnect will further reduce our ability to lead communities in need of direction. People in community place as much credence in their relationship with their leader as in the leader's knowledge. In this new time, when one path looks as good as the next, trustworthy relationships become even more important. A postmodern individual will not follow simply because a pastor claims to be speaking truth. Pastors are but one voice for a generation that hears numerous "authorities" claiming various "truths." Members of that generation will not test these truth claims by conducting double-blind experiments on scientific data, nor will they blindly accept the propositions of religion simply because an institution says its tenets are true. Postmoderns weigh truth claims by sensing whether they can trust their relationship with the one who purports to know the truth. Fortunately we follow a leader who placed a high priority on honest relationships.

We can influence the searching souls of our day, but not with the methods of modernity—no matter how well they worked in the past. Attempting to hold on to the past hinders our present relationships and reduces our opportunities to influence the future. This danger of a rearview vision can be found even in the use of the term "postmodern." Though it is a useful descriptor, reminding us that a certain era is past, "post" suggests that we are looking back. Until we move beyond describing our time by what was, we will not be able to define what will be. Effective leaders learn from the past and operate in the present, but they realize that their most important task is to create a constructive vision for the future.

Openings and Obstacles to Community Leadership

The good news, for those willing to assume the risks of leadership, is that times of upheaval offer as much opportunity as they do frustration. Imaginative leaders thrive in times of disorder because they recognize disruption as a precursor of transition. Pastors in touch with their own and others' fears and frustrations can simply empathize with and provide pastoral care to people caught in the grief accompanying disruption (a valuable but limited ministry), or they can provide a broader and more prophetic ministry by pointing to the prospect of God's working through times of turbulence. Such leadership can be a challenge to those of us who were taught that empathy and care are the hallmarks of a good pastor.

Fortunately, systems theory has been added to our basic pastoral-care training. We now realize that congregations and communities are systems, and that when a system is disturbed, the people within it (often including the leader) will work diligently to stabilize it. Only when we move beyond denial and discover that the old homeostasis cannot be restored will we become more open to adapting to the new reality. Leaders fluent in systems theory seek to do more than calm a disturbed system. They strive to understand the underlying causes of the discontent and to help those within the system see beyond emotional reactions. These leaders help people understand both the risks and the rewards of change and lead them through the transition to a positive outcome. Although we who serve as pastors tend readily to empathize with our congregations and communities as they grieve change, we will have to give more than empathy: to be their leaders, we will have to do the hard work of understanding the causes of disruption within the systems and to find new responses to help these systems rise to the challenges of a new day.

As difficult as it is to retool our congregational systems, it is even harder for pastors and congregations to engage the systems of their local communities. Congregants rightly remind us that the bulk of our responsibility lies in our congregations, but the primacy of these tasks does not preclude community leadership. In fact, we have a responsibility to help our congregations see that they are one system amid many, and that each system affects all others. As we will see in chapter 3, both pastors and congregations have a calling to minister to both congregation and community.

The mission of retooling local communities to deal with the complexities of postmodernism cannot be accomplished by working exclusively within the confines of our congregations. Our sphere of influence as pastors has grown too small, and we no longer have the needed trust of the majority of people who live and work near our churches. As one pastor put it, "My congregation is located on a major thoroughfare. While I preach to a couple of hundred people, I watch 10,000 drive by, not caring in the least what I am trying to communicate." If we are truly to effect change, we will have to reengage the people who work and live in our communities. One way to do that is to lend our leadership to the organizations that are having the most impact locally. Though other civic-minded people may share their much-needed skills and gifts with our communities, pastors have a unique calling and skills that few others can offer. In particular, postmodern people struggle with two issues that clergy are uniquely equipped to address: meaning and ethics.

Interpreters of Meaning and Morality

Questions of meaning, or basic existential pondering (Why am I here?), are part of what makes us human. Ontological questions (Who else is here and what is my relationship to others or to the Other?) naturally follow. As cultures shift, the answers accepted by one generation do not always satisfy the next. Historically, religious leaders have not only provided answers to questions of meaning but have also helped people to reframe their questions and even to ask new ones (to question the questions). In the bygone era of modernism, as people sought answers to questions of meaning, authority to address those questions—that is, to lead—was granted to those who possessed critical "knowledge," whether scientific, medical, religious, legal, or whatever. What the leader knew and the solutions the leader offered often determined the value of his or her leadership. If companies had "quality issues," they consulted a quality-control expert. If they had safety issues, they hired a safety officer. Leaders, in an effort to set themselves apart from other knowledgeable people, began to develop proficiency in increasingly specialized areas.

Similarly, pastors began to move from being generalists to specialists—religious educators, pastoral counselors, and youth ministers, for example. Like our secular counterparts, we became well informed in specific areas, and our expertise became our calling card. In a postmodern era, however, people no longer lack information—they are overwhelmed by it. Almost anything you want to know (even about preaching, pastoral care, or congregational organization) is available through multiple resources (24-hour cable TV networks with specialized programming, the Internet, and the thousands of newspapers, magazines and books published each year).

The expert's access to facts is no longer a source of authority. Authority lies rather in the ability to interpret data meaningfully. The details a physician learned in medical school are available on the Internet with a click of the mouse. A doctor's credibility lies not in access to medical information, but rather in the ability to interpret a wealth of data, to diagnose the presenting symptoms, and to prescribe the proper treatment. Similarly, a pastor's place in the community depends not on bringing a congregation or community some new "Bible knowledge" (Google can find Bible verses faster than most of us), but on interpreting the relevance of the faith's ancient teachings to contemporary issues. Communities don't need one more source of data, but they hunger for guides who can interpret vast quantities of information and who can help move us toward deeper questions about meaning. Knowing the facts is not as valuable as understanding which facts are important and how to apply wisdom to a real-life situation. As pastors we have the opportunity to teach the biblical distinction between knowledge (understanding facts) and wisdom (proper use of knowledge).

As people committed to the search for meaning, pastors are prime candidates to step into the morass of data and to provide leadership to overwhelmed communities. We don't have to have all the answers, because asking the right questions is as important as finding the answers. Ask a few good questions that help people find meaning in the hodgepodge of community living, and every leader in town will welcome you. Our communities usually suffer not from a lack of information but from a lack of leaders with both knowledge and wisdom. Given the amount of information generated daily, we have an even greater need for "meaning-makers." Leaders who possess both knowledge and the wisdom to sort out and apply knowledge exert greater authority now than in the past.

Wise pastors can exert great influence in postmodern times because the search for meaning manifests itself most profoundly in the way postmoderns reflect upon ethics. We may feel that we have lost influence because in modernity (and to a greater extent in pre-modernity) preachers could espouse ethical codes with the expectation that society would accept and attempt to follow those edicts. In postmodernity, a few followers might continue to heed our advice, but the great majority do not hear our words and even question the authority of pastors to preach to them about ethics.

Such a development is painful, but not necessarily negative. Perhaps it is time for pastors to join academics and others in critically examining traditional systems to provide more solid grounding for moral decision making in a postmodern era. The postmodern apologist Zygmunt Bauman confronts us with this assertion: "If philosophers, educators, and preachers make ethics their concern, this is precisely because none of them would entrust judgment of right and wrong to the people themselves or would recognize, without further investigation, the authority of their beliefs on the matter."[5] When faced with challenges to our authority, our first inclination is to try to prop up our support and to appeal to our position (about which postmoderns care little). Such positional authority, however, is weak when compared to relational authority. We can better serve both community and congregation when we move from behind our pulpits and into the midst of the people facing today's moral dilemmas.

Moving out from behind the pulpit and into the community will place us more in line with the ministry of our Lord. Jesus walked among the people and often challenged the propositional ethics of his time with more relevant questions of morality lived out in relationship to God and neighbor. Perhaps the greatest example of Jesus's moral teachings is the Sermon on the Mount, which warns, "Unless your righteousness surpasses that of the Pharisees and the teachers of the law, you will certainly not enter the kingdom of heaven" (Matt. 5:20). Here Jesus challenged his hearers to move beyond external, behavioral regulations to explore deeper concerns, their motivation. He pointed out that the people of a community are more important than the laws regulating community: "The Sabbath was made for man, not man for the Sabbath" (Mark 2:27).

It can be tempting to join the Sadducees and Pharisees in issuing ethical decrees to communities that seem to have forgotten how to distinguish right from wrong. The Christian tradition, on the other hand, recognizes that external regulation (which seeks to coerce behavior) cannot change the heart or produce guidance for unforeseen dilemmas. Even when such coercion seems to work, it tends to produce minimum expectations, and even these lowered expectations cannot be sustained outside the power of the enforcer.

In contrast to external control, motivation that emerges from the core of one's being is both coercion-free and self-sustaining. For instance, marital fidelity based on fear of the consequences of being found unfaithful is less meaningful than fidelity rooted in mutual love, respect, and trust. Though an approach that examines motivation as well as behavior has always been beneficial, it is even more important in a time of competing ethical systems. While other postmodern leaders may choose to ignore factors of motivation, it is a vital question for Christian leaders. When postmoderns examine clergy claims to leadership, they look for more than lists of do's and don'ts; they seek a comprehensive rationale that offers guidance in a changing, if not chaotic, world. Serving as leaders in today's climate requires us to have an ethic that is not tied to one culture or time but that transcends both culture and time.

As hungry as postmoderns are for companionship and guidance in their search for meaning and a coherent, relevant ethic, they will not simply accept the word of clergy or other leaders.

They will first test the leader's authority—for example, by watching how our leadership plays out in the broader community. Postmoderns value both persons and community. Unfortunately, many have not experienced healthy communal systems, nor do they automatically choose to define community in traditional ways (as evidenced by the state of the family and the decline of other community institutions, such as congregations). Many are left without external guidance (as taboos of society have fallen, for better or worse) and without internal guidance systems.

I heard of a recent community college commencement at which the speaker assured the graduates that they knew the difference between right and wrong. A friend who teaches ethics at that institution questioned the validity of the speaker's assertion. From his classes, he recognized that the excessive emphasis on individualism in recent decades has left many students with no comprehensive foundation for moral decision making. What we see as a lack in postmodern ethical preparedness, however, may be an opening for pastors and faith communities. When postmodern people encounter ethical dilemmas, they often seek direction from many sources. Though this generation rejects authoritative moral assertions, its members are open to pastoral guidance that respects both their experience and their value as persons.

The pastoral guidance that most ministers feel comfortable exercising one-on-one or in a small-group setting is needed in dealing with wider communities. Just as a pastor might use a series of exploratory questions to help a congregant move past concerns about rules and regulations to explore basic motivation and consequences of action, so too a pastor can help a community explore shared concerns in greater depth. One might achieve this aim by writing a thoughtful op-ed piece on the ethical consequences of the expansion of a local industry or by serving on a medical ethics advisory board at a local hospital. As a pastor becomes involved in local leadership (by serving, for example, on a chamber of commerce committee), the small-group settings offer the opportunity to engage in for-mative dialogue on a variety of issues before they reach the community at large (at which time they often become more convoluted).

Like congregations, community systems are experiencing a metamorphosis and need the help of those with the wisdom to guide groups in meaningful discussion leading to productive action. Neighborhoods, towns, and entire regions are search-ing for leaders to help them move past divisiveness and to envi-sion a positive future. When we dare to venture into these conversations, we challenge many people's perceptions of pas-tors. Such acts redefine the pastoral role and afford us the op-portunity to make a greater difference within our society.

Hesitance to Engage in Community Leadership

Despite new opportunities as well as historical precedent for clergy to provide community leadership, many pastors are not certain that they can serve as leaders in the wider community. Given the turbulent times, the role is a challenging one. Caught in the gap between a quickly changing culture and a slow-to-change church, we are tempted to spend most of our energies mediating the crises in our congregations. Our congregants clearly need us, and we are most comfortable working within the realm of our training. Moreover, the pressures of cultural change can overwhelm, and we wonder if we can truly influ-ence the forces buffeting congregations and communities. We easily overreact by moving to one of two extremes—either battening down the hatches to preserve cherished traditions or redesigning our entire ministries in an effort to become more relevant to the culture. If we try to hide in tradition, however, we deny the reality of a new day's challenges, further disconnecting ourselves from our changing communities. This disconnect widens the gap between congregation and community, lessening our ability to lead in the community. No one wants a leader who doesn't understand reality. On the other hand, if we attempt to catch up to culture by constantly redesigning our ministries, we will find that culture changes faster than we can adapt; then we become followers of culture, not leaders of congregations and communities. A third option is to deny neither our heritage nor our culture, but to challenge and engage both in an effort to find the best in each.

A New Understanding of Culture

Though postmodern culture seems at odds with our congregations, one cannot assume that contemporary culture is anti-Christian. In fact, postmoderns highly value spirituality and are open to new apologetics based in relational rather than rationalistic understandings of faith. (Such an approach sounds a lot like incarnational theology). Postmoderns do not reject Christianity so much as they reject what appear to be culturally bound expressions of Christianity. This is not to say that openness to spirituality will always lead to an affirmation of the Christian faith. As with all who hear the message, some will choose to follow Christ; others will not. It is to say, however, that many postmodern people are open to God's working and seek honest interpretations of their experience. When confronting the spiritual milieu of postmodernism, we might take a clue from Paul's response to the people of Athens (Acts 17:16-34).

Instead of immediately criticizing their idolatry, Paul first affirmed their search for truth and then shed light on a new way of experiencing God—through Jesus Christ.

Like all converts, new Christians shaped by a postmodern culture bring a great deal to the church. In my congregation we are sometimes guilty of wanting to reach younger people to meet our own institutional needs rather than to reach out in compassion to meet *their* needs. What we often desire from the next generation is a new workforce to perpetuate our traditional institution. However, institutional goals do not usually win the commitment of postmoderns, nor do they call forth the best that postmoderns have to contribute. Though we may not wish it, postmodernist converts can bring much-needed renewal by challenging our previous cultural understandings of the faith. The postmodernist emphasis on trustworthy relationships as the foundation of community is a good corrective for those of us who focus much of our energy on programming as the foundation for community. Postmodern Christians challenge us to examine our faith practices so that we might "distinguish between church traditions and the Christian Tradition, and move emphasis from the former to the latter."[6]

Christianity's Offerings to Postmodernism

Suggesting that postmodernism has correctives to offer to our practice of Christianity is not to suggest that Christians should be uncritical of the culture. Christianity has more to offer postmodern culture (or any culture, for that matter) than postmodernism has to offer Christianity. First, in this transitional time Christianity offers the vast insights of a faith that has engaged in meaningful dialogue with evolving culture for more than 2,000 years. Ours is not the only day in which some have sought to dismiss Christianity as an irrelevant belief system that has outlived its usefulness. From its inception, Christianity has both struggled with and given guidance to culture.

Shortly after the dawn of the early church, Nero attempted to make a political scapegoat of Christianity, but the faith outlived the empire. Similarly, in the cultural clashes of the late Middle Ages, when the church was again being co-opted for political means, Christianity survived the political distortions and emerged more influential than any ruler of that day. In the aftermath of the eighteenth-century Enlightenment, when Auguste Comte and other philosophers summarily dismissed religion as the superstitions of a bygone day, Christians continued to believe and to find direction from their faith. Surviving 2,000 years of history does not necessarily prove Christianity's benefits. But multiple generations of followers have found its basic tenets a trustworthy guide in numerous cultural settings; that history gives us hope that we who represent the faith today can be relevant leaders to our generation.

Second, the ethical underpinnings of Christianity avoid the extremes of externally enforced moral dictums (which don't always translate to new situations) and individualistic relativism (which gives little guidance in times of transition). Drawing its core from the life and teachings of Christ, who modeled healthy relationships within community, the gospel offers postmoderns authentic ways of living within community. The core of Scripture upholds the primacy of relationship and the consequences of our actions upon relationship. Even areas of Scripture that might seem more focused on external control, such as the Ten Commandments or the Pauline epistles, have as their goal preventing the breaking of relationships and restoring broken relationships. The first three commandments deal with our relationship to God and the last seven with our relationship to others. The pinnacle of Paul's writings is 1 Corinthians 13, which argues the primacy of love in all relationships. Though postmodern listeners might conclude from some of the preaching of our day that Christianity is a religion of peripheral pronouncements, we have the opportunity as we engage our communities to correct this misperception in word and deed. By focusing on the core of our faith, we provide an alternative ethic that can reaffirm the postmodern emphasis on relationship while offering a corrective to rampant individualism.

Third, in a chaotic era, we offer a hope that can bring meaning and order to both individuals and communities by focusing on the development of a positive relationship to God and neighbor. Christianity's resurrection focus serves as a corrective to both those who take life too lightly (an attitude refuted by the cross) and those who would fall into despair (a state of mind refuted by the resurrection). In a day of fleeting commitments and shallow relativism, our faith offers an ethic that rejects both licentiousness and legalism as we engage our communities. Our faith offers a response to postmodern folks' hunger for relationship by providing an ethic that focuses on the importance of relationship with both God and neighbor.

At the same time, this ethic offers a prioritized order for relationship. Christianity encourages us to focus first on our relationship with God, and then to use the grace we find in this bond to build relationships with those around us. Thus we move past relationships of convenience (what can we do for each other?) to relationships of meaning (what do we mean to each other?). As postmoderns face thousands of choices daily, most driven by consumerism, Christian hope points them past relativism, which has few concerns of value, to a method of decision making based on the value of relationship. As meaning is then found in relationship with others and with the Other, this new way of ordering life begins to restore the hope that there is more to life than this current culture.

Fourth, we have a tradition that offers stability in a chaotic world, while allowing the incorporation of fresh insights and practices from each new generation (so long as they don't contradict core beliefs). For instance, our faith has allowed (though sometimes painfully) adaptations to worship styles. Whether one worships with an organ, a band, bongo drums, or no instruments at all, the object of Christian worship is more important than its form. In a world where many want to keep their options open, while longing for stronger foundations, our faith does not require postmodern people to reject openness to the future to become part of a faith with deep roots. In fact, Christianity offers a faith oriented toward a glorious future—one that will be brought about by God but also one in which we have an opportunity to participate. As we step into our postmodern communities, we can relate a tradition that not only embraces newness, but also declares a God who makes all things new. If our culture is looking for something new, it might find it, ironically, in a faith that is old. As we seek to lead in this time of transition, we offer our communities both the benefit of a historical foundation and the hope of a new day.

Diverse Views of Christianity and Culture

H. Richard Niebuhr's classic work *Christ and Culture* reminds us that discerning how to be people of faith in a changing culture is not a new issue. The rate at which culture changes has accelerated greatly since the turbulent 1960s, but Christian congregations have struggled since the time of Christ to live out their faith within their culture. Niebuhr points out that people of faith have often taken extreme positions, either rejecting culture ("Christ against culture") or embracing culture ("Christ of culture"). In the first view, Christians focus on an unseen world yet to come that is at war with the world in which they live. Those who take this view run the risk of focusing so intently on a world to come that they become totally detached from (and often hostile to) the world in which they live. Detachment and hostility create such a distance between these Christians and the contemporary culture that most people begin to see such Christians as irrelevant. In the second view, people of faith see Christ as "a great hero of human culture."[7] Those who take this view run the risk of losing their unique voice through total accommodation to culture—a form of irrelevance itself.

In response to these extremes, Niebuhr offers other alternatives,[8] concluding with a middle ground of "Christ the transformer of culture." Such a view is critical of culture but also hopeful. In fact, it emphasizes the need to develop bridges to the contemporary culture. Christ is seen as the redeemer of a good but corrupt culture, and Christ's followers are to work in the power of the Spirit to continue redeeming God's creation. The view that Christ and the church transform culture has an obvious lure, which seemed to work for centuries with the expansion of Christendom. The decline of Christendom and the rise of postmodernism, however, have proved that transforming culture to fit within the values of faith is more difficult than it might seem.

It is ironic that congregations that viewed themselves for decades as transformers of culture have shifted the way they relate to culture as the culture has shifted. Many have unconsciously moved from an attempt at transforming culture to the preservation of a particular culture, Christendom. In our efforts to preserve what we think is "good" and to guard what we know is sacred, we have moved to a passive form of the "Christ against culture" stance. Not wishing to "fight" culture, as our more conservative brothers and sisters tend to do, we simply withdraw into our congregations. We are like bears hoping to find a cave in which to hibernate until the harsh winter subsides. We hope to arise one day into a glorious spring, even if we have to wait until Christ returns to accomplish the work we were not able to do—to transform the culture to reflect our understanding of God's values.

Our problem is that this withdrawal disconnects us from those to whom we seek to minister. Our "hibernation mentality" tells the world we are asleep and makes us of little consequence to anyone outside our "congregational cave." The net result is that we leave unfulfilled our commission to "go into all the world." Unchurched people might occasionally drop by our worship services, but they leave feeling as though they have entered a time warp or encountered a historic relic. Certainly they will not think they have found assistance for living in a shifting culture.

Moving beyond the Disconnect

Those within our congregations also sense this disconnect between their congregation's mission and the culture it is called to serve. Our more honest parishioners will occasionally remind us that, though they appreciate our pious sermons, they must live in the "real" world the rest of the week. They might enjoy a nostalgic time-out from a confusing culture, but they soon hunger for guidance to help them deal with that culture. A parishioner recently told me of visiting her childhood congregation to attend a homecoming celebration. The pastor preached a long, strenuous sermon against the evils of going to dance halls. It made her laugh as she looked around and imagined her 93-year-old mother and the other women in the congregation, many closing in on the century mark, going to dance halls long defunct. The pastor was preaching against culture—but against a culture long past. Out of kindness, our parishioner decided not to confront this pastor. She didn't want to disturb the fantasy that he and his congregation were still living in a simpler time, since she knew they lacked the resources to confront the much more difficult issues of today. Failing to examine the relevance of our own congregations, however (whether out of kindness or fear of what we might find), is ultimately no "kindness" at all. Such an approach will not, in the long run, contribute to the overall health, vitality, and faithfulness of a congregation or its community.

It is not an illusion, however, that many in our culture think most pastors and congregations live in a fantasy world. I have been disturbed by this perception in both urban and rural settings. When I lived in Atlanta, I was shocked (in my naïveté) by the response of a neighbor when I tried to persuade him to visit our congregation because our ministry was important to the community. "Burger King thought it was important to the community too," he said, "but that didn't make me want to eat there." Having my congregation compared to a fast-food restaurant was unnerving but enlightening. Like the neighborhood Burger King, that Atlanta congregation also closed. Despite the pain, I began to wonder if there might be lessons for our congregations and communities in the opinions of those who seemed not to care about a church's presence in the community. Perhaps congregations, small businesses, and even local communities share the same challenges in the face of substantial cultural shifts.

Moving from Atlanta to rural northwest North Carolina, I hoped for a better appreciation of the value of congregations within local communities. Though I found a more "churched" culture (folks called me "Preacher" on the street, though my pastor friends told me it was more of a warning to others than a greeting to me), I also found many who thought that congregations and pastors were out of touch and had little to offer. This attitude showed itself quickly in my first attempt to provide community leadership. As I mentioned earlier, our county was dealing with the need for new facilities for several schools, and a bond referendum was being considered. I wrote and mailed to the chair of the school board a "basic campaign strategy" designed to rally our community around education to pass the referendum.

She was impressed with the proposal and shared it with a group of community leaders who had formed an ad hoc committee to promote the referendum. When one member of the group, an influential local businesswoman, read the proposal, she didn't believe a pastor had written it. I'm told she said something like this: "How could he have written this? He's only a preacher, isn't he?" She and I are good friends today and have worked together on many educational initiatives, but that doesn't change the fact that, even in well-churched rural areas, many have to be convinced that pastors and congregations can offer relevant leadership to their communities.

The feeling that pastors are out of touch has been exacerbated by the clergy's reluctance to adapt to postmodernism, but to some extent this prejudice against adapting to our culture has always been present. People expect clergy to take a "Christ against culture" stance and will even help "protect" us from the stain of secular society. They like having us on the shelf as nostalgic reminders of a simpler day, and we enjoy pretending that Christendom is still in power. We miss the times when culture and congregations walked hand in hand. Gil Rendle makes this point in his video presentation "Living into the New World: How Cultural Trends Affect Your Congregation." Rendle says, "Back then it was a cultural expectation to be involved in a congregation. Even those who didn't attend church, if asked, would say that they did."[9] We liked it when people felt an obligation to come hear us preach—even if they had to lie about it! As country music group Rascal Flatts sings:

> Well, I miss Mayberry,
> Sittin' on the porch drinking ice-cold Cherry Coke.
> Where everything is black and white.[10]

Or as *Baptists Today* editor John Pierce comments, "There is something appealing about living in Mayberry, where values are widely shared and no problem takes more than 30 minutes to overcome. There, everyone shows up for worship at the community church—and even Otis Campbell [the lovable town drunk] dries out by Sunday morning."[11] Despite these wistful longings for simpler times, we all know that Mayberry was just a television show and, as one who lives 45 miles from Mayberry (Mount Airy, North Carolina), I can assure you that even Mayberry is no longer "Mayberry."

For one who grew up in those simpler days of Christendom but who serves as a pastor beyond them, it is still easy to become nostalgic—despite the fact that I've spent a lot of time thinking about cultural change and how I and the congregations I serve should respond to it. I feel especially nostalgic about the place of the pastor in local community leadership. While I was in seminary in Louisville, Kentucky, professors regaled us with stories of a time when no community leader (business or governmental) would consider making a major decision without consulting the Catholic bishop and the pastor of Walnut Street Baptist Church. Upon hearing this claim, I went to visit Walnut Street Baptist Church and found a graying congregation struggling to minister in an inner-city environment. As I talked with a few of the members, however, I was reminded of the congregation's proud heritage and was assured that the stories my professors told were true. I wish I could serve as a pastor in a community like bygone Louisville!

Though similar conversations about how members can participate in community leadership take place in my ministry, they are fewer and farther between. It has been my experience, and that of my closest peers, that relatively few civic, political, or business leaders seek us out before making major decisions affecting our communities and congregations. Of course this is a two-way street, and we pastors, who tend to be highly focused on our congregations, are also less likely to take the initiative in making contacts with community leaders.

While we might grieve this loss of contact between pastors and other community leaders, its recognition gives us an occasion to evaluate and refine our leadership within our communities. We need to be honest about our nostalgia and, as good counselors, recognize that our yearning, like all emotions, colors our perception of the situation and keeps us from moving forward. For instance, white southern pastors might feel nostalgic about the influence they held during the 1950s, but if they focus only on the joys of that era, they will miss the recognition that not everything was splendid then, and that not everything new is detrimental to faith communities. One might want to ask an African American or female pastor what leadership he or she was afforded in bygone days and reflect on the gifts and skills these pastors, who were once prevented from sharing with the broader community, now bring for us all to enjoy. In Christendom, culture may have tipped its hat to religion, but faith communities paid a price as some not-so-Christian cultural values were forged in the partnership.

Alban Institute founder Loren Mead describes some other subtle ways the alliance between Christendom and modernity negatively affected the faith. In *The Once and Future Church*, he notes that the lack of separation between world and church removed hostility from the environment, but it also united sacred and secular—a partnership that moved mission to far-off enterprises and stripped the congregation of its local mission.[12]

The church and culture were never really one, but the fantasy that they shared much in common met needs for both, giving little impetus for congregations to challenge the delusion that both the culture and their communities were relatively Christian. And as long as we believed that our culture was Christian, we had little work to do in it, a perception that shifted our focus to foreign mission fields—where we tended to export our culture along with our faith. We believed that little mission work was needed at home (except among groups that had not accommodated to our culture—such as Native Americans).

So instead of carrying out mission and ministry at our doorstep, we focused on promoting and preserving Christendom. After all, Christendom gave special place and power to clergy. Rarely, however, was this power used to call into account a Christian culture that was not always so Christian. When a few ministers joined with civil-rights leaders in the 1960s to challenge the institutional sins of racism and violence in our culture, many of those ministers lost their "cultural grant" of leadership in their congregations and communities.

This is not to say that they could no longer provide *any* leadership. In fact, those who stood up against culture were sometimes able to lead other groups of concerned citizens to institute changes that had a greater and longer-lasting impact than the efforts of clergy who held onto their traditional roles. These few "radicals" redefined leadership around their message instead of their leadership position. One need look no further than Martin Luther King, Jr., to see that someone rejected by "cultural Christianity" can still exercise local, national, and even international leadership. On the other hand, pastors who failed to engage local and national cultural issues, electing instead to maintain cultural norms, saw their ability to influence cultural challenges dwindle.

As we can see, that Christendom fell is not all bad. At its core, Christendom failed to remain "Christian" and no longer deserved the support of the church. Theologians and ecclesiologists Stanley Hauerwas and William H. Willimon make this point when they argue in *Resident Aliens* that the fall of Christendom is a positive development:

> The demise of the Constantinian world view, the gradual decline of the notion that the church needs some sort of surrounding "Christian" culture to prop it up and mold its young, is not a death to lament. It is an opportunity to celebrate. The decline of the old Constantinian synthesis between the church and the world means that we American Christians are at last free to be faithful in a way that makes being a Christian today an exciting adventure.[13]

In response to the demise of Constantinism, Hauerwas and Willimon invite Christians to become "resident aliens" and our congregations to become "Christian colonies." Certainly there is biblical grounding for this view. Being "resident aliens" sounds much like Jesus's prayer for his disciples, "not that you take them out of the world but that you protect them from the evil one" (John 17:15). The terminology also captures the sentiment of Christians who feel like aliens living in this postmodern world. At the same time, "resident" reminds us that we are to be present in the world as bearers of the truth of Christ. We may be alien to this culture, but we do not have the luxury of withdrawing from our communities. What better way to represent the "Christian colony" than to lend our leadership as ambassadors of the colony? We participate in community leadership not to produce a Christian culture (recognizing that there is no such "social order" outside the fullness of God's glory), but rather to be faithful witnesses amid the brokenness of our communities. What Hauerwas and Willimon describe as an exciting adventure sounds like a thrilling opportunity for leadership.

New Opportunities for Community Leadership

Though I have described the diminished frequency of conversation between pastors and community leaders, I am always thrilled when such an opportunity presents itself. Because the culture in which we live no longer automatically recognizes the potential leadership of clergy, I know that these conversations are not simple courtesies but real opportunities for dialogue and influence. It was in such a conversation that I recognized what I had been learning for some time—that congregations and communities share a symbiotic relationship.

When I arrived 10 years ago at First Baptist Church in North Wilkesboro, North Carolina, I was invited to have lunch with Mayor Conley Call. This was no surprise because he was also a deacon in our congregation. What surprised me was what

Conley wanted to share. "Pastor," he said, "The health of our town and the health of our church go hand in hand. When the town does well, the church does well. When the church does well, the town does well. We need each other." Conley then went on to describe the tremendous challenges facing our community and how they correlated to the numerical decline of our congregation.

I soon found this new confidant to be both hopeful and realistic. He is well aware of the predicament of small towns, but he is also engaged in finding solutions to these complicated problems. He continues to challenge me to see that God is working in more quarters than just in our congregation. Through example and encouragement, he and others have shown me not only the importance of the relationship between congregation and community but also that community pastoral leadership is still possible.

Though providing community leadership as a local pastor is possible, it is not easy. The issues that face both congregations and communities are not easily solved. The partnership between congregation and community is no longer a given. This reality, however, does not alter the importance of the relationship, nor does it diminish the need for pastors to exercise leadership within both. Though various communities are dealing with different issues, all are undergoing transformation and long for leadership to guide them along the journey.

We might be tempted to give into despair and to say that we live in a post-Christendom era that affords us little opportunity to exercise influence. Certainly the fall of Christendom means that we are no longer automatically granted a seat at the table of power. But it does not automatically exclude us from a table that has more seats than leaders to fill them. The opportunity for pastors to step forward and earn community leadership can be one of the most positive results of postmodernism. Redefining the pastor's place in community through earned leadership is not only possible: it has the potential to transform our congregations and communities.

Chapter 3

Prophets, Priests, and Kings

A Biblical Model for Pastoral
Community Leadership

Christian pastors are inheritors of the early church's leadership practices. Leaders were designated as needs arose, particularly as the community grew and became more complex. Names for early leadership roles tended to describe particular ministries rather than designating formal offices. First-century Christians used a host of terms, with both sacred and secular origins, to describe their leaders, including *episcopos* (bishop or overseer), *presbyteros* (elder), *diakonos* (deacon/minister), *didaskalos* (teacher), *poimen* (pastor/shepherd), *euangelistes* (evangelist), *epostolos* (apostle), *prophetes* (prophet), and *liturgos* (public minister). Authority wasn't drawn from titles so much as titles were given to those who held certain skills or knowledge. The apostles held the most authority, because they had known Jesus. The apostles, however, could not supply all of the leadership needs.

While Christianity was quickly growing, the ranks of the apostles were shrinking with every death, and leadership roles and structures began to shift. Congregations were planted by itinerant prophets and evangelists, but they were nurtured by pastors, elders, and deacons. Some congregational leaders who showed extraordinary ability became leaders of leaders, as bishops or overseers. Because these leaders were developing structure for an emerging faith, it might seem as if they had to make it up as they went along. Fortunately, early Christian leaders were not starting from scratch. Because Christianity emerged out of Judaism, Christian leaders were able to draw from the best of Judaic leadership practices and organizational structure.

As we seek to meet age-old congregational expectations while meeting contemporary community needs, we can follow the examples of early church leaders. The apostles and other leaders drew strength from their Judaic roots, while redefining the leadership models of prophet *(nabi)*, priest *(kohen)*, and king *(melek)* to fit their understanding of a new work of God. This process of reshaping leadership roles was neither overt nor quick. Instead, roles evolved as Christian leaders began to understand that the practices of an established faith could not adequately express the message of an emerging faith. On the positive side, building on leadership models from Judaic practices gave theological grounding to first-century Christian leaders. On the negative side, no single model from Judaism could fully communicate what Christian leaders saw as the pinnacle of revelation—the ministry and message of Jesus the Christ. New wine could not be contained in old wineskins. Therefore, they often followed the lead of Jesus, who adapted the best of each of these historical models to relate to a new day.

Unfortunately, this practice (drawing models from an established faith to help define an emerging faith) created confusion as Christian leaders used terms similar to Judaic language in dissimilar ways. To further compound the confusion, Christian leaders began to cross cultural barriers rarely traversed by Jewish leaders. This willingness of Christian leaders, such as Peter and Paul, to evangelize Gentiles was one of the stress factors that eventually led to Christianity's formal break with Judaism. These new converts, however, added more than numbers to the church. Gentile believers brought a cultural viewpoint not seen in purer Judaism. The resulting debates, concerning Hellenistic influences, challenged Christian leaders to find a way to move even further beyond the borrowed language of Judaism to express the basic tenets of Christianity to an entirely different culture. Knowing that the leaders of the early church were able to cross cultural barriers while retaining the integrity of the faith gives comfort to those of us who face a similar task today—leading congregations to engage an emerging culture without losing basic truths.

Perhaps we can take a clue from the apostles and other early church leaders, who followed Jesus's example of both embracing and expanding on the Old Testament models of prophet, priest, and king. Jesus borrowed from the servant psalms of the prophet Isaiah to define the nature of his ministry while pronouncing that he was the fulfillment of Isaiah's prophesy (Luke 4:16-21). The writer of Hebrews describes Jesus as not just a priest, but as a high priest in the order of Melchizedek who would complete the law (Heb. 7:15-20). And Matthew's Gospel takes great pains to identify Jesus not only as the rightful inheritor of the throne of King David, but also as its redeemer (Matt. 1). Just as Jesus and the biblical writers reinterpreted these traditional leadership roles to explain Jesus's work among us, so early church leaders pushed their images of leadership even further in response to their own need to conceptualize and practice a new kind of leadership that reflected Jesus's self-emptying love.

First-century Christian leaders began the task we continue today—developing and defining leadership practices capable of guiding the Christian faith. As we seek to expand our leadership beyond our congregations into our communities, we can learn much from our early church predecessors. Like them, we realize that our skills and knowledge give us more of a base of leadership than our position or title does. We can also derive much wisdom from Old Testament leaders, who operated out of personal (knowledge of God), professional (skill in ministry), and positional (power of office) authority as prophets, priests, and kings. I find both the strengths and pitfalls of each role instructive for my own leadership, and I believe we can learn much from them about how to serve as Christian leaders in the wider community.

Multidimensional Leadership

Drawing insight from the experience of bygone leaders to influence congregation and community has advantages and pitfalls. The examples of how prophets, priests, and kings related to their respective communities give pastors a variety of leadership methods to connect with our communities. For instance, when dealing with economic hardship we might choose to function as prophets (truth tellers) and speak out about economic disparities that are being ignored or accepted as status quo. Or we might choose to function as priests (counselors and keepers of rites) by calling those within our sphere of influence to pray for those in need, offer aid from our wealth, and repent of systemic sins that hold others down. Or we might choose to function as kings (stewards/administrators) both by focusing the resources of our congregations to create new opportunities for those in need and by using our influence on other kings (modern-day power brokers) to encourage them toward the same kind of activity.

Unfortunately, trying to operate out of multiple leadership models can make a pastor seem a bit scattered. Should we spend what little time we have serving in the soup kitchen or soliciting the funds to endow the soup kitchen? Should we spend the day driving a recently unemployed parishioner to job interviews or use our time to serve on an economic-development commission seeking to increase the number of available jobs? Should we encourage our parishioners to spend their time, energy, and economic resources to address community-wide issues, or should we call them to use their resources to strengthen struggling ministries within our own congregation?

Such questions, however, do not always have to have "this or that" answers. We can often find "both/and" solutions. By choosing to serve one weekend a month (instead of every weekend) in the soup kitchen, we can share firsthand the importance of the ministry to potential donors while being good stewards of our limited time. Likewise, if we lend our leadership to community economic-development efforts while finding a retired parishioner to drive unemployed members to their appointments, we will have more inroads to connect our out-of-work congregant with potential employers. And encouraging parishioners to connect with the larger community increases their awareness of resources beyond the congregation, resulting in more efficient use of resources for both congregation and community.

In drawing upon the biblical roles of prophet, priest, and king, however, we need to guard against narrow interpretations of biblical role models as "this or that" types of leaders. Unfortunately, in an effort to clearly describe models for preaching (or publishing), we sometimes oversimplify the way men and women of old lived out their callings. We stereotypically see prophets as "anti-establishment" tellers of truth, priests as "practitioners of sacred liturgy," and kings as "royal builders and defenders of communal structure."

When we restrict our understanding of these faithful leaders to one dimension of their ministry, however, we fail to comprehend their depth as people of God who faced a variety of challenges. In fact, most biblical leaders were required to fulfill not one but several roles. Prophets were not always the confronters of the status quo. Isaiah was clearly a royal counselor; he probably learned the ways of a priest from his priestly family. Priests did not always operate strictly within the confines of temple worship. Samuel both anointed royal leaders and chastised them for their errors. And, while kings functioned as war leaders and administrators, they were also perceived as instruments of divine revelation. David, as king, led Israel to restore the Ark of the Covenant to a prominent place in the nation's worship.

Exploring more deeply the lives of Old Testament leaders yields additional evidence that they did not always make neat distinctions between the seemingly contradictory roles of prophet, priest, and king. When Hezekiah ruled Judah in the eighth century B.C., the prophet Isaiah was given open access to his court. Even when Isaiah had predicted King Hezekiah's death, Hezekiah called upon the prophet for counsel and healing. Isaiah then used a cake of figs to help heal the king. Hezekiah acquired 15 more years of life and Isaiah received an even greater place of influence (2 Kings 20:1-11). The fact that Hezekiah is remembered as one of the few "good" kings of Israel has much to do with the king's willingness to listen to God through the voice of the prophet. Priests too exercised leadership outside their expected liturgical duties. When the overlords of the Seleucid kingdom of Syria began to overtax the Jewish community, force their captives toward foreign practices, and then loot the Temple, it was a priest who began the revolt. Once Matthias refused to offer a heathen sacrifice, choosing instead to fight, many other Jews began to rally around his leadership. Matthias and his sons quickly consolidated the resistance and took on a protective role that in times past would have been reserved for a king.

Viewing biblical leaders holistically, rather than one-dimensionally, provides a firmer basis for understanding effective leadership in our own century. We need to recognize prophets, priests, and kings as people with diverse backgrounds, talents, and personalities, who because of their calling and setting tended to operate in certain ways. Prophets tended to be people of passion who felt deeply about people's suffering and God's wrath toward the wickedness that caused such suffering. Therefore, they were apt to speak passionately about moral concerns—as did Amos when he confronted the Northern Kingdom.

Priests also felt deeply about the hearts of the people but tended to approach the problem from a different angle. They worked within the religious system and therefore were more likely to seek gradual change through their daily liturgical functions. For instance, Aaron gave shape to a formalized liturgical system that greatly helped Moses mold a loose-knit coalition of tribes into a nation. And many kings shared the concerns of prophets and priests regarding the lives of their people. Kings, however, tended by virtue of their office to function as builders, decision makers, and regional protectors. Saul and David rallied the people around military might, while Solomon was known for his wisdom and accomplishments in foreign policy. Though prophets, priests, and kings operated in different ways and in different venues, the Bible refers to all of them as God's anointed leaders.

Finding the Right Leadership Stance

As men and women called by God to leadership today, we often function in ways similar to prophets, priests, and kings (though our "kingdoms" are very small). Like priests, we are to "comfort the afflicted." Like prophets, we are to "afflict the comfortable." And to accomplish these competing tasks, we often need the wisdom and resources of a king.

Distinctions among the roles can be as fluid for us as they were for our ancestors in the faith, and as community needs arise, we can draw equally on the leadership examples of yesteryear's prophets, priests, or kings. Whether challenge, comfort, or counsel is needed, a pastor who is known as a caring presence within the community will have opportunities to lead.

For instance, when the unthinkable happened on September 11, 2001, I was meeting with a group of business people, politicians, and educators discussing the link between economic development and education. Like all Americans, we immediately went into shock as we watched the video of the planes crashing into the World Trade Center and the Pentagon, replayed again and again on network and cable TV. Almost immediately, the group turned to me and asked for a prayer. I am sure that in the days following this national tragedy, many clergy were called upon in various settings to use their priestly gifts to comfort their communities. On a smaller scale, similar calls for leadership are extended every day—whenever communities encounter difficulties.

If we—like the prophets, priests, and kings of biblical days—offer comfort and counsel to our neighborhood and community, we too will have opportunities to lead beyond our congregation and denomination. If we move beyond congregationally bound prophetic preaching about economic injustice to actively lending our support to community-wide economic-development efforts, we might begin to alleviate the suffering of the unemployed and underemployed. If we not only provide priestly benevolence, but also seek to understand

and join others in addressing the root causes of poverty within our communities, we might not have to provide so much food, clothing, and shelter. And if we engage other community leaders in wise conversation, we can expand our influence as a significant voice among the "kings" who govern us and protect us today. Given the declining influence of clergy, finding opportunities to lead in our communities may be more difficult than it was for the prophets, priests, and kings of Israel, but it is no less important than it was in their day. We are called by God to be leaders, but more important, we are called to become Christ incarnate outside the doors of our church.

The Example of the Prophets

Although the challenges facing today's leaders might seem far removed from those that biblical leaders had to overcome, the lessons they offer are more relevant than we might think. Certainly the prophets, who often faced openly hostile audiences, have much to teach us. Robert Cate, the Phoebe Schertz Young Professor of Religion at Oklahoma State University, observes, "Perhaps the most amazing feature of the Hebrew prophets was that they were tolerated at all."[1] Yet their words and actions continue to challenge us today.

In seeking a biblical grounding for community leadership, we do well to remember that prophets did not become leaders through taking on a formal position but rather because they were appointed by God and they trusted God to validate their message. As Cate continues, "The very fact that they survived and that their messages were kept and passed on is a measure of the awareness of the Hebrew people that they did in fact hear the voice of God in the words of the prophets."[2] Prophets did not just "grab" leadership, though it might appear so, but spoke a message so full of God's truth that it compelled many to follow. What allowed prophets of old to lead in times of uncertainty was their faith in the One who gave them their message. Thus they felt compelled to lead whether or not anyone followed.

Their calling from God to lead in difficult times did not mean that the prophets always wanted to step forward in leadership. Like those of us who serve as pastors today, prophets were often reluctant messengers. Before Isaiah answered God, "Here am I; send me!" he first cried, "Woe is me. I am ruined!" (Isa. 6:5-8). Jeremiah argued, "I do not know how to speak; I am only a child" (Jer. 1:6). Ezekiel's call, with an eerie windstorm containing fiery wheels and convolutions of human and animal faces, would have frightened most of us. No wonder he had to be told, "Do not be afraid, though briers and thorns are all around you and you live among scorpions" (Ezek. 2:6).

Daniel was called to lead, despite being a captive in a strange land. Hosea suffered the humiliation of marriage to an unfaithful woman, a situation he eventually used as a sermon illustration. Joel was asked to step forward amid the devastation of a plague of locusts. Amos was a shepherd called to confront kings. And Jonah, perhaps the most reluctant of all prophets, ran away from his call and thereby ended up in the belly of a fish. All of these prophets, however reluctant, eventually confronted their communities (or the communities to which they were sent), thus providing leadership amid the challenges of their day.

Of these "reluctant" leaders, Jeremiah stands out as one who truly struggled to share a message he did not wish to speak. Known as the weeping prophet, Jeremiah did not enjoy the harsh words he was called to preach to his people. Jeremiah instead rejoiced when God changed the message to one of hope and restoration. Jeremiah's purchase of a field at Anathoth, paying full price while the Babylonians were at the gates, is one of the most powerful and hope-giving acts of community leadership of all times. As God's leaders for today, we can take both example and hope from the biblical model of leadership provided by the prophets. Like those of old, we too are called to pronounce both God's truth and God's gracious hope in challenging times. Remembering the dimensions of prophecy, confrontation, and comfort will help pastors of today develop a model of community leadership that avoids the extremes of condemnation and capitulation.

Another lesson to be learned about community leadership from biblical prophets is their paradoxical relationship with their communities: they were in communities but also spoke independently from their communities (a situation similar to Stanley Hauerwas and Will Willimon's concept of resident aliens). Though the biblical record's lack of information about most of the prophets' backgrounds might make it seem as though prophets appeared out of nowhere to confront their communities, this lack of introduction does not necessarily prove they were always strangers within their context. In fact, many of them were already involved in leadership. Larry Gregg, pastor of Calvary Baptist Church in Rutherford, North Carolina, notes that at least some prophets, such as Nathan, held "semi-official" court responsibilities:

> While he emerges from nowhere in the biblical narrative, Nathan functions harmoniously over time with the monarchy in the announcement of the Davidic dynasty (2 Sam. 7:1-17) and the determination of David's successor (1 Kings 1:1-40). This harmony does not appear to have been interrupted even by Nathan's denunciation of David for his adultery with Bathsheba and subsequent murder of Uriah (2 Sam. 12:1-25).[3]

Gregg further illustrates the close relationship between prophets and kings by pointing out that in Scripture "often the names are paired: Saul and Samuel, David and Nathan, Ahab and Elijah, Hezekiah and Isaiah, Jehoiakim and Jeremiah."[4] This Old Testament relationship between prophet and king provides another biblical precedent (and perhaps model) for pastoral community leadership. The prophet was both involved with the political leader of the community (at least in reminding him or her of God's desires) and independent of the political leader. They exercised a leadership style I refer to as "detached involvement." Gregg puts it this way:

> What distinguishes these personalities [the prophets] in contrast to their contemporaries [the court prophets], who also bore the title *nabi*, is their independence. While closely associated with their respective monarchial protagonist, they are not institutionally "housebroken." Their ears are attuned to the voice of YHWH and their mouths forth-tell the pronouncements of God. This sets them apart from sycophantic court prophets of the time who simply uttered what the king wanted to hear.[5]

If we are to follow this model of engaging our communities as prophets, we will do well to participate in community leadership while maintaining the independence needed to speak words of caution when necessary.

Unfortunately many have either misinterpreted what it means to be prophetic or have given up this aspect of our pastoral ministry altogether. The lack of a prophetic voice is showing itself in a lack of leadership in our communities in part and in our nation as a whole. Many pastors have decided that being "prophetic" means declaring God to be on one side or another of a moral debate. Consequently, they have sold out to partisan politics (of either the right or the left), choosing to focus on one or two issues, while overlooking other of God's priorities. Genuine prophecy, however, does not trap God into one view or another, but recognizes God's transcending power to change the view of all. When God speaks, it is usually not to say that one is right and another is wrong, but to point all to a higher ethic.

On the other hand, because prophecy can be so difficult, other pastors have abandoned the prophetic role and have dropped out of civic leadership altogether. Whether we sell out to a single cause or totally abdicate our prophetic responsibilities, the result is the same—God's voice is not heard in our community or culture. As Jim Wallis, editor of *Sojourners* magazine, reminds us:

> The loss of religion's prophetic vocation is terribly dangerous for any society. Who will uphold the dignity of economic and political outcasts? Who will question the self-righteousness of nations and their leaders? Who will question the recourse to violence and the rush to wars long before any last resort has been unequivocally proven? Who will not allow God's name to be used to simply justify ourselves, instead of calling us to accountability?[6]

The questions Wallis raises are important ones that must be answered. Making the example of the prophets a vital piece of our community leadership is a step in the right direction.

The Example of the Priests

Prophets serve as biblical models somewhat related to, but more independent of, their community; their call was often to "shake things up." Priests, however, serve as biblical models of people more closely related to their community—models whose call was often to restore order and to preserve the community. Priests were practitioners and keepers of liturgical tradition. Their temple duties served as ritual reminders that God had acted in the past, giving Israel hope that God would provide for the future. Reidar B. Bjornard, professor emeritus of Old Testament interpretation at Northern Baptist Seminary, points out, "In biblical studies it is customary to underrate the priests in favor of the prophets. However, it is probably fair to say that if it had not been for the faithful work of generation after generation of priests, the prophets would have had no congregation to address."[7]

While some prophets were closely connected to specific kings, as noted above, prophets in general had a somewhat conflicted relationship with the monarchy. The priestly system, however, was structured during the royal period, and priests often established their authority in the very courts of the monarchy. Bjornard notes: "At the time of the return from exile, the people had a High Priest, who according to the prophets Haggai and Zechariah, was equal to the prince in power and status. And because Judah never again obtained a king, the high priest, for all practical purposes, was the leading person in the nation, something we see substantiated during the time of the Maccabees and at the time of Jesus."[8] Thus priests not only provided community leadership but also at times were *the* designated community leaders.

Although Jesus is often seen as at odds with the priests of his day, he does not attack their right to lead but rather their failure to lead in the right way. Jesus, like several Old Testament prophets, condemned those who prioritized ritual over relationship by warning, "And you experts in the law, woe to you, because you load people down with burdens they can hardly carry, and you yourselves will not lift one finger to help them" (Luke 11:46).

Though Jesus's words are harsh, they are also an expression of a higher expectation of leadership. Jesus expected the priests of his day to do more than maintain ritual. Jesus understood that the purpose of ritual was to remind people of God's gracious acts of the past and to give them hope for God's gracious intervention in the present. Jesus wanted priests to use their liturgical duties to lift burdens from the people instead of making ritual just one more cumbersome chore. When we as religious leaders look at the burdens many carry within our local communities, we too need to remember that whatever leadership standing we have is to be used to help relieve these burdens. Certainly there are times when we need to take a prophetic stance against abuses we see in our community, but we need to temper our prophetic words with priestly reminders of God's grace through the ages.

Both prophets and priests were called to live among the people as representatives of God, but it was the work of the priests to find ways of helping the people to remember God's grace long after the prophets had spoken. At times the presence of prophets and priests demanded that the people recognize God's call to justice and righteousness in community life. At other times it communicated the comforting, sustaining love of a gracious God to a hurting people. In some instances we might step momentarily into leadership to speak a sharp truth that demands immediate action. At other times we might become more intricately involved in the process of helping our communities interpret, remember (ritualize), and live out God's truth. In either case, when in our own communities we see those who are hurting economically, socially, physically, or spiritually, our call as God's leaders is to help lift these burdens.

Certainly we can exercise priestly leadership through the ministries of our congregations and larger ecclesiastical bodies. We dispense words of challenge and grace each Sunday, we offer redeeming ritual to those who attend, and we work with other Christians to provide charity. But we can be more effective in communicating God's grace and providing help for all when we form partnerships beyond ecclesiastical circles and cooperate with other community leaders and agencies.

In my own community, our congregation has been concerned about the large number of workers displaced by companies outsourcing jobs. Because some of our members work at the local community college, where displaced workers are being retrained for other work, they have been able to help us identify specific needs of these hurting people. We learned through our members that although federal funds related to the North America Free Trade Agreement (NAFTA) provide economic resources for outsourced workers to attend the community college and to retool for a new economy, these funds are not sufficient to provide for the daily needs of many families. To help these workers remain in school rather than taking lower-paying jobs to provide for the immediate needs of their families, our congregation has concentrated our benevolence funds on providing for the daily needs of some of these at-risk families. Without our congregation's connection to the college, we would not have been as clear about the needs of these families, and our help would have been much less efficient.

The example of the priests shows us how to preserve our sacred calling while working with secular leaders to meet the needs of the people. Our best example of this partnering might be Ezra. Though there are many textual and historical problems with Ezra and Nehemiah, and it is no doubt an idealized account, we can still learn from the story. As a gifted scribe,

Ezra not only helped preserve the Torah while in captivity but also used his skills to make himself valuable to government officials. When time came for the return from exile, he was commissioned by the Persian authorities to help bring about order in Jerusalem. Together with Nehemiah, another Jewish leader who had gained prominence in the Persian court, Ezra began literally to restore the foundations of the community. Ezra reminded the people of God's law, and Nehemiah directed the rebuilding of the city walls. Both directed and encouraged the workers in the rebuilding of a city's infrastructure, economic system, and governmental organization.

When I find myself feeling out of place in a community meeting about the need to provide the water and sewer infrastructure to accommodate a business's job expansion, I remember Ezra and Nehemiah partnering to rebuild a city. The willingness of the priests of old to work with those beyond the religious establishment to lift the burden of people more effectively gives us a positive example for expanding our ministries beyond the confines of our congregations.

The Example of the Kings

Few pastors will have the opportunity to participate in direct municipal governance, but we can still learn from the example of Old Testament kings who protected their people, united their kingdoms, settled disputes, and managed communal resources. Unfortunately, most of us have a romanticized view of kings developed by watching a few too many Disney movies in childhood. Knowing how biblical kings operated, however, will help us in both our congregational and community leadership. Most pastors at one time or another have to protect the congregation's integrity, unite people behind a shared vision, calm troubled groups, and stretch limited resources. What we may not realize is that government officials and business leaders face these same tasks and are often open to the help of other leaders. Kings need both royal advisors and the example of other wise rulers—both roles that a pastor can fill.

The primary responsibility of any governing power is to protect its people. Joshua led the people to possess the Promised Land. To guard the people from invaders, leaders (known as judges) were raised up; they organized defenses and protected the people's claim on the land. Israel's first king, Saul, did not disappoint those wanting a strong military leader who would protect them. He proved himself to the people by winning battles against the Ammonites, the Philistines, and the Amalekites. Despite his great conquests, however, Saul ultimately lost his own family and his sanity—reminding us of the propensity of power to corrupt.

While we should heed this warning, it should not stop us from using what power we have to protect all of the people (especially the powerless ones often forgotten by government). As we earn leadership opportunities in our communities, we gain the standing to speak to other leaders about the need for justice; that is one way we can begin more effectively to protect those for whom we are responsible. For instance, when one of my pastor friends learned several years ago that our county commissioners were refusing to fund a certain charity while giving themselves a raise, he decided to take action. He simply wrote a letter to them on church stationary, "innocently" pointing out this inconsistency. Amazingly, he got a call two days later explaining that there had been a mistake and that the funding had been found for the charity.

A second responsibility of governance is to unite. We live in days when consumerism, self-concern, and competition for limited resources make it difficult to promote the common good. However, we are not the first people to experience tumultuous times, nor are we the first who have tried to help individuals and groups to see that we function better together than apart. Strong leaders reach beyond themselves and across conflicts to focus us on communal welfare. For instance, amid the corruption of Saul's reign, which produced divisiveness and civil war, a unifier arose. Through a combination of military power and restraint (especially concerning the failings of Saul and his family), David united both Judah and Israel. Though David, too, later fell to the corrupting influence of power, the Jewish people long to this day for a nation as unified as the 12 tribes were in David's day.

We will probably never bring unity to an entire community, but we can strive for the common good and encourage other leaders to do the same. Many pastors possess the gift of casting a vision for a better day. If we can expand our vision beyond unifying our congregations to unifying our communities, we will be in step with the best that royalty has to offer.

One of the community efforts that moved me beyond my congregation was a community-wide "visioning" process started by the chamber of commerce several years ago. What first caught my attention was a newspaper article in which our community's consultant used the biblical-sounding language of vision, values, and unity. The articles invited the people of our community to attend town-hall-type meetings where we could share our hopes and concerns with various civic leaders. I decided to attend. It was exciting and energizing to participate as we discussed our problems and brainstormed solutions.

Watch what you do and say, however: my enthusiastic participation gained notice, and I was tapped for leadership. While I started out as head of a committee on educational improvement, today I chair Wilkes Vision 20/20, a program that involves matters as diverse as quality of life, sense of community, cooperation in governance, private-sector leadership, infrastructure expansion, economic development, and school improvement. To help our community move toward our goals in these areas requires that other leaders and I constantly promote a shared vision and a sense of unity.

A third responsibility of governance is legal adjudication, which requires the wisdom of a king. Solomon, of course, is remembered for such wisdom. Most of us learned as children the story of Solomon threatening to cut a baby in half to determine which of the two women who claimed the child was truly the mother (she was the one willing to give up the child to preserve his life). Solomon's wisdom, however, was much greater than this, and he proved himself in areas as diverse as architecture, economic development, and foreign policy.

Unfortunately Solomon, like all of us, did not always show wisdom in his actions, and much of the progress he brought about produced negative side effects: heavier burdens on the people and the corruption of the monotheistic faith. Although we are once again reminded about the corrupting influence of power, we can still strive to exercise wisdom by seeking the welfare of all in our communities.

In a recent church facilities committee meeting, one of our deacons asked a number of interesting questions that began with "What if . . . ?" "Have we thought about . . . ?" and "Isn't there another way to look at this?" I thanked him after the meeting for helping us to explore more options and for leading the discussion to a deeper issue (we moved from rules for building usage to the purpose of having church buildings). He replied, "That's my job at work too. I'm the 'what-if' guy." He went on to explain that businesses value those who are able to help the group consider all the options, explore the consequences of actions, and ensure that personal motives are not driving decisions. He noted that thinking through these issues, rather than making hasty decisions that might have to be reversed, saves time and money.

As I said in chapter 2, many pastors also possess a similar intuitive inquisitiveness and are particularly good at asking questions that open up unexplored options and expose underlying motives and meanings. Though we might feel that we have little wisdom, when we allow the King of kings to lead us in asking questions that help our communities explore options, think through consequences, and examine motivations, we are drawing upon the best of our royal predecessors.

A fourth responsibility of governance is ensuring the proper stewardship of shared resources. Josiah showed just such ingenuity when he realized that, though Judah had limited resources, it could play a key role in world affairs. Josiah maximized Judah's defense capabilities by aligning with Babylon to overthrow the dominant Assyria. In doing so, Josiah was also able to rid the nation of Assyrian religious cults and to invest resources, which had been supporting a false religion, in repairing the Temple. Because of his ability to maximize limited resources and to bring revival to the land, Josiah became one of the most praised biblical kings. As 2 Kings 23:25 records, "Neither before nor after Josiah was there a king like him who turned to the LORD as he did—with all his heart and with all his soul and with all his strength, in accordance with all the Law of Moses."

Unfortunately, most local governing bodies are finding their resources stretched as well. Though pastors today might not be able to turn two fish and five loaves into a meal for thousands (as happy as that would make both congregational and civic leaders), we have worked with limited church budgets for quite some time and can bring our experience to bear in the wider community. As I have worked with others in my community to steward our resources, I have learned as much as I have taught.

During my time on our local United Way board, we have faced shrinking funds and growing needs. To address these problems, we have learned the techniques of "outcome-based management." Outcomes are simply measurements of whether we are truly making a difference by funding certain programs. Though I have said jokingly that outcomes-based management means, "It is no longer good enough just to do good," I recognize that the real issue is "how to make the most impact with limited resources." Knowing that we can't do it all, I have learned to ask, "Where can we invest our limited time, energy, and financial resources to make the most difference?" Joining with others in community leadership has proved to be a wise use of my limited resources, as it has given me the ability to influence the stewardship of even greater resources.

Learning from the example of biblical kings can be empowering for pastors, especially for those who have not been as comfortable with this model because of misunderstandings about power. Pastors have tended to avoid the kingly role for a variety of reasons. First, the leadership models most of us learned in seminary stressed either the priestly (pastoral care) or prophetic (preaching) role. Second, all of us know at least one pastor who has misinterpreted the kingly role and assumed an authoritarian posture that proved harmful to a congregation. Third, most Protestant congregations are still fearful of hierarchical structures and find ways to remind pastors that we are to be servants first. And fourth, we have misunderstood the role of king by failing to understand how a king's skills of protecting, unifying, negotiating, and managing can aid the work of our congregations and communities.

If you choose to lend your leadership within your community, however, I hope you will be as pleasantly surprised as I have been that those outside of our congregations often help to bring out the best in our royal blood. In a world where power is more openly expected and exercised, a pastor's exercising a little authority doesn't raise as many eyebrows. Though the servant-leader model of Jesus remains a primary model for pastors, we will do well to remember that Christ also drew heavily upon the models of prophets, priests, and kings.

Avoiding Extremes in Community Leadership

It is easy to find both historical and contemporary examples of clergy operating primarily from their interpretation of a singular biblical role model. Pastors who feel called to address slipping moral standards often focus on the prophetic model and tend to become moral crusaders. Clergy who feel strongly about the needs of people see themselves as channels of God's benevolence and can develop into extreme priests. And, while a few clergy have sought to improve their communities by seeking public office, many others have acted like little emperors, seeking either to co-opt the powers of the state for their own purposes or to build rival "kingdoms" in which they can exercise complete control. In each case, the role becomes negative when taken to an extreme, although the purpose of the role itself is positive. Effective pastoral community leadership draws from the strength of examples of the prophets, priests, and kings, both to give leadership options in various settings and to allow the strengths of each model to temper the extremes of the others.

Moral Crusaders

Moral crusaders, whether they are like the apostle Paul blasting the evildoers of Rome (Rom. 1:16ff) or Jerry Falwell forming the Moral Majority to stop "America's descent into paganism," are concerned about the ethical standards of their communities. Unfortunately many moral crusaders hold a narrow view of what it means to be moral, choosing to focus on issues that they think are important but that are often divisive in the community. Believing strongly that they are right, moral crusaders are rarely open to dialogue and can be combative. Obviously, the attitude of the moral crusader creates problems. People who take on the role tend to judge others with a list of "pet sins," while ignoring our universal need for confession and forgiveness. They are often antagonistic, driving away the ones the minister seeks to influence. Consequently, moral crusaders tend to cut themselves off from others by digging trenches for warfare instead of building bridges for peace.

We have good reason to challenge these extreme prophets about the nature of their ministry. Because moral crusaders tend to be passionate, and many other pastors have taken a passive stance toward their communities, at times the crusaders have become the dominant voice among community pastors. Unfortunately, the crusaders' dominance means that, in some communities, the attacks of moral crusaders have led leaders from outside the church to view all pastors negatively.

To offset this influence, pastors with a more balanced approach to community leadership must offer a counterpresence as well as challenge those among their colleagues who use extreme, one-dimensional models of leadership. It is easy to find examples of Jesus confronting the moral crusaders of his day, reminding them, "Do not judge, or you too will be judged"

(Matt. 7:1), and "First take the plank out of your own eye, and then you will see clearly to remove the speck from your brother's eye" (Matt. 7:5). In following Jesus's prophetic example, however, we need to be extremely careful in how we confront moral crusaders—lest we too fall into this trap of usurping God's place as judge.

Despite the combative nature of moral crusaders, which poisons the leadership environment for other pastors, these people might have a corrective for our leadership as well. One leadership quality they possess—and that some of us lack—is passion. They address (even if in a bellicose manner) what they see as the ethical concerns of their day. Any time one seeks to lead in a community, whether sacred or secular, morality and ethics (how we relate in community) are important issues. Although their confrontational nature tempts us to dismiss moral crusaders, let us not repeat their error of dismissing people for taking a position different from their own.

Fortunately, at the local level, moral crusaders often are not permitted to label others with simplistic stereotypes. When you truly live in community, people get to know pastors and other leaders as human beings, aside from their station in life, so that stereotypes and unfounded attacks tend not to stick for long. For instance, shortly after my arrival in North Wilkesboro, North Carolina, our youth group came up with an idea to fund its mission trip: members would donate money to see one of our church leaders kiss a pig! Unfortunately for me, most of our people would rather see their pastor kiss a pig than to witness any of our lay leaders or other staff members doing so. Word soon spread that the pastor of First Baptist Church was going to kiss a pig in front of the church after Sunday services.

That morning, as I drove into town, I happened to catch one of our radio preachers who enjoys playing moral crusader.

Believe it or not, I was his illustration for the day. Although he didn't refer to me by name, he clearly stated that the city pastor was busy kissing a pig while our community was going to hell in a handbasket. Luckily for me, both kissing a pig and having this pastor rail against me won the hearts of many people in our community because they recognized that the new pastor had a sense of humor. Although moral crusaders can create a negative environment for other pastoral leaders, they fortunately tend to show themselves for what they are.

Though being ridiculed by a radio preacher seemed funny to me, moral crusaders can be both hurtful and harmful. Unfortunately, many have misunderstood prophecy to be moralistic diatribes. This type of speech is hurtful because it tends to devalue others instead of lifting them up to see a better way. It is harmful to the ones at whom the speech is directed because it replaces true prophetic words, whose purpose is always healing, with personal judgment, whose purpose is often demeaning. And it is harmful to the cause of Christ because the techniques of moral crusaders often cause defensive reactions in others, raising barriers to the work of God's Spirit.

As a friend of mine recently said, "Just because you get in somebody's face and scream at them doesn't make you a prophet!" Or as the true prophet Micah says, "And what does the Lord require of you? To act justly and to love mercy and to walk humbly with your God" (Micah 6:8b). Prophecy is not about making judgments but about causing change. As Bob Hulteen, associate editor of *Sojourners* magazine, puts it, "The crux of misunderstanding is this: Prophecy is not the result of seeing into the future. Instead, prophecy is the faithful declaration of the implications of current actions on the future, with the hope of having an impact on both."[9]

We cross from being prophets to being moral crusaders when we forget that prophecy is not about our personal moral judgments but about God's call to a higher ethic. Keeping a check on our tendency to condemn others, by remembering that Christ said, "Judge not, that ye be not judged" (Matt. 7:1 KJV), is a good practice in community leadership. If we become seen as vindictive or unwaveringly on the side of one group or the other, we lose our prophetic voice and the opportunity to make a difference for all. Jim Wallis explains that religious people approach public life in one of two ways—moralistically pronouncing that God is on our side or asking (like Lincoln) the more important question, "Are we on God's side?"[10] Wallis notes:

> Those are the two ways that religion has been brought into
> public life in American history. The first way—God on our
> side—leads inevitably to triumphalism, self-righteousness, bad
> theology, and, often, dangerous foreign policy. The second
> way—asking if we are on God's side—leads to much healthier
> things, namely penitence and even repentance, humility, re-
> flection, and accountability. We need much more of those,
> because they are often the missing values of politics.[11]

Wallis is not suggesting that Christian leaders withdraw from civic leadership. Rather, he is reaffirming our call to genuine prophetic leadership.

How then are we to become effective prophets in our communities without slipping into the role of moral crusader? Several other questions point the way. First, are we proclaiming a higher message that promotes community by reflecting the Old Testament prophets' and our Lord's call to peace, justice, humility, and love? If our message is more a personal attack than a call to community, we have become moral crusaders. Second, are we acting out of anger that reflects a self-righteous attitude, one that violates the sacredness of others, or are we displaying a humble, broken heart, one that reflects an understanding of our own sinful nature? If we are enjoying the message, we have probably left the circle of biblical prophets who spoke reluctantly after dealing with their own anger so that they might speak words of both warning and hope. And third, will our words help others see a higher truth, producing the fruits of repentance and change? Or will they escalate tensions, blocking others from hearing that truth, and further breaking community?

If our words do not open opportunities for transformation, then we have simply condemned instead of offering a path to hope and healing. Being true prophets of God is an awesome task requiring us to proclaim a higher message than our own, rise above personal vendettas, and offer a grace beyond our ability.

Extreme Priests

If moral crusaders go to an extreme in one direction, extreme priests go the other. Extreme priests overemphasize the care ministry and often are seen as little more than chaplains to the establishment. They are asked to pray at civic gatherings because they won't offend anyone and, if asked nicely, might even offer up a nonsectarian prayer. Although these ministers are seen in their communities as nice folks, they run the risk of making all pastoral leaders seem a bit like ecclesiastical window dressing for special occasions only. Too often extreme priests, in an attempt to relate to people, become accommodators of culture instead of representatives of the Christian faith. These ministers "know the right people," but if they fail to give guidance to those with whom they mingle, what leadership are they providing? In an attempt to be gracious, extreme priests can settle for adding a religious veneer to secular activities.

Though extreme priests enjoy the remaining vestiges of Christendom, often serving as chaplains to various clubs and organizations, serving in these capacities does not necessarily make one an extreme priest. Many in these jobs provide a valuable ministry. Certainly chaplains for hospitals, police forces, fire departments, the military, and the like have opportunities to minister in the most difficult of situations. My friend Paul Hugger, who serves as our hospital chaplain, has the opportunity to minister to a broader cross-section of our community than any other pastor I know. Another of my friends, who has served as a U.S. Navy chaplain, leans paradoxically toward pacifism. He is, however, one of the few ministers I know who has been given the opportunity to preach a message of peace within the chapels of ships of war.

The difference between extreme priests and effective community pastors can be seen in their fruit. Extreme priests derive pleasure and benefit from public positions but fail to use their position to speak a word of prophecy or a call to community stewardship. Effective community pastors balance their figurative blessing of the community groups they serve with prophetic challenges of behavior and calls to higher administration of the group's resources.

I must confess that I relate better to those who become extreme priests than I do to those who lean toward becoming moral crusaders or little emperors. Given my personal tendencies, it can be a real challenge for me to provide both care for my community and an authentic witness to the Christian faith.

As a minister who tends to "err on the side of grace," I sometimes find myself feeling used by people who simply want a rite of the church without a relationship to a congregation. I have officiated at more than one wedding for couples who had been turned away by what I assumed to be "less caring" clergy. It's always my hope that these couples will respond to the grace offered by becoming a part of what I view as a loving congregation. A few do, but I continue to be disappointed that most of these couples (having gotten what they need, "the ceremony") have had little to do with our congregation. Alas, for their purposes, a wedding in our church sanctuary simply provided an attractive backdrop for a "photo op"—or, worse, a "video op." Moral crusaders are not the only ones with blind spots.

Pastors who sit at the elbow of those with power need to be careful that their access to power doesn't blind them to their responsibility to challenge earthly powers as well. If we hesitate to challenge power when it is misused, we become extreme priests indeed. As a local politician recently expressed one aspect of the dilemma as she considered her vote on a controversial issue: "If I do what I think is right, I probably won't get re-elected. If I lose my position, how can I make a positive change in our community?"

Her pastor's response is one that pastors who cozy up to authority might also need to hear. He advised, "If you judge each vote on whether or not you can remain in power, it won't matter how long you serve: you'll never make a difference!" Similarly, if a pastor who has access to authority never challenges that authority, for fear of losing access, he or she will never make a difference either. What good is having a voice with the powers that be if we never use our voice? The politician had nerve enough to vote her conscience, and to her surprise, others took courage from her stand and joined in defeating the measure.

When pastors with access to authority are willing to speak both affirmation and challenge, they give courage to the one they are trying to influence. The strength of those of us drawn to the role of extreme priest is that we tend to be both present and caring. However, without critical reflection about what we are offering, we can become little more than religious window dressing.

Little Emperors

The weakness of pastors who seek to become little emperors has been shown throughout history. When religious leaders have gotten too cozy with those who hold the power of the state, both state and church have been weakened. The abuses of the Crusades, which continue to have ramifications today, are a clear example of the dangers of the attempts of religious leaders and monarchs to use one another. The church wanted to restore the Holy Land to Christendom, and European princes and kings wanted to expand their power and territory. As a result, the church and state formed an alliance in which neither checked the abuses of the other. Extreme violence was done in the name of the One who rejected the use of violence. The message of salvation was lost in the method of salvation. And, in the end, neither church nor state achieved its goals—spreading the faith of the church or expanding the territory of the state. Such is the result whenever church and state attempt to blend sacred and secular goals.

As religious leaders, we might assume that our nation would be better off if clergy were to use the powers of the state to enforce a more moral society. The Inquisition, however, shows what can happen if we follow that line of reasoning. Here again, those who said they were following the Prince of Peace began to do violence in his name. This time, instead of killing "infidels," they turned on those who also confessed the name of Christ. The results were not much different from those of the Crusades. A faith that grew through voluntary conversions was turned into one of forced compliance. Instead of unifying the church in doctrine, the use of state-endorsed violence further split the fellowship.

After the Reformation, too, Protestant reformers did no better as little emperors than the Catholic leaders who had carried great power before them. For instance, John Calvin had no qualms about issuing a death warrant for Michael Servetus over a conflict about the doctrine of the Trinity. It is ironic that many of those who would like to use the power of the government today to dictate morality in the United States fail to see that such an arrangement would create in America a system identical to those regimes they abhor—the oppressive religious control seen in the states of the Middle East and elsewhere around the globe.

Seeking to align with earthly kingdoms, however, is not the only way pastors can become little emperors. When clergy become power-hungry and are denied political control, they often seek to build their own kingdoms. These little emperors tend to confuse building *the* Kingdom with building *a* kingdom. Often they are people with great charisma and good intentions; unfortunately, they tend to develop ministries more reflective of their own personalities than of the work of Christ.

Although we might laugh off the excesses of people like Jim Bakker, he possessed great influence over thousands of people. More tragic examples are David Koresh, the Branch Davidian leader who led people to their death in a conflict with the U.S. government; Jim Jones, whose Jonestown community in Guyana came to an end when he coerced his followers into a mass suicide-murder; and other cult leaders who created whole societies under their direct control. Although these examples of little emperors are severe, they point out the dangers in becoming enamored of power and personal desire instead of God's desire for genuine community.

This is not to say that clergy should refrain from seeking to influence those who govern. A few among our ranks have even felt the calling to expand their ministry through public service. Though seeking elected office is not an aspiration of most pastors, even those of us who are not called to such work need to be more public in our ministry. We will never effectively confront unjust systems or be available to help communities in crisis if we are unwilling to work both behind the scenes and in front of the people. If we have failed to exercise our public-ministry muscles by working side by side with other community leaders, we may be too weak to respond when needed. However, we must undertake such ministry with humility, remembering that the Lord granted Israel a king only reluctantly and that Jesus rejected those who wanted him to build an earthly kingdom. We are not called to build little kingdoms (whether within our congregations or communities), but to build up the Kingdom of God.

An Effective Community Leader

To be an effective community leader, a pastor will need to draw upon the strengths of all three biblical roles—prophet, priest, and king. Like prophets, we must speak words of truth and hope for the betterment of all. Like priests, we must find ways of reminding people of God's gracious presence in all circumstances.

And like kings, we need to protect our community, unite others for the common good, seek solutions to conflicts, and encourage the wise use of communal resources.

Effective community pastoral leaders also remember that the prophets, priests, and kings of Scripture were multidimensional leaders who used a variety of approaches to build their communities. Though they might have approached leadership by playing to their strongest gifts, biblical leaders also allowed God to stretch them in new ways or to rely on the strength of other leaders. Prophets could be found in the courts of kings, both giving counsel and receiving support. Priests showed that they recognized God's leadership in the words and actions of prophets and kings by recording their speeches and commemorating their actions in Scripture and liturgy. And wise kings included other voices in their courts, often relying on prophets and priests for outside counsel. To be effective in community leadership, we too will have to approach situations from various viewpoints and to recognize the strength of working closely with other leaders.

When biblical leaders became one-dimensional, Scripture records how God used one type of leader to balance the excesses of another. The priest Jethro advised Moses (who for all practical purposes was serving as a royal figure) to decentralize his power for the welfare of the people and himself. The prophet Nathan issued a stern rebuke to a corrupt King David. And kings, on rare occasion, disciplined an errant priest (1 Kings 2:27).

Our ultimate example, however, of effective leadership comes from Jesus. As noted earlier, Scripture describes Jesus as a prophet, the King of kings, and a priest after the order of Melchizedek. In fulfilling these roles, he challenges false prophets, confronts the crass attitudes of the priests of his day, and reminds rulers of their limited power. To show a different way, he spoke prophetically by pointing to the intention behind the law in the Sermon on the Mount. He faithfully carried out the work of a priest by offering up his own life in sacrifice. And he proved to be the King of kings by always putting the welfare of the Kingdom above his own.

Though we will never attain Jesus's skill in effectively balancing the leadership examples of prophets, priests, and kings, we can still seek to lead as our leader led. Jesus rejected one-dimensional leadership in favor of drawing from a variety of the rich experiences of his heritage to face differing leadership challenges—and so can we. When Jesus needed to help his disciples remember God's presence, he instituted a new priestly ritual—Holy Communion (Matt. 26:26-30). And, as a good king, he unified people through a vision while providing for his people's physical and spiritual needs (Matt. 6:33).

In following Christ, we too will have occasion to carry out our various roles as prophets, priests, and kings. Deciding when and how often to lean on each role can be difficult for leaders. When I took driver education in high school, though, I remember some advice our instructor gave that might be a helpful guide for balancing these roles. He told us that we could judge whether we were driving a reasonable speed by observing how many people we passed versus how many people passed us. He suggested that the numbers should be about the same. To achieve a balanced biblical approach to community leadership, I suggest that we track the number of times we function as prophet, priest, or king. Given our various settings, we might lean toward one (especially if we are already inclined toward that stance), but effective leadership requires that we use the best of all three roles.

Like the prophets, we need to listen for God's message for our community, remain observant of harmful behavior, and speak truthful words that both warn and lead to a better way.

When Jesus observed oppression and injustice, he openly challenged the leaders of his day, issuing woeful warnings and calling them "whitewashed tombs" whose inner lives needed to be renewed (Matt. 23:27). Like the best priests, we need to move past simple liturgical duty and fulfill our calling as intercessors for the people before God and interpreters of God's word to the people. Jesus properly interpreted the law—which others had turned into a legalistic burden that only they could rightly discern—pointing toward a higher ethic of love understandable to all (Matt. 5). And as kings, we need to emulate the most effective practices of ancient kings, who at their best properly placed God's will above their own desires and served faithfully as guardians of the people's welfare. Jesus set aside all glory to live a meager life, which he also gave in full, to make the riches of the Kingdom available to all (Phil. 2:5-11).

As we seek to lead by emulating Christ's ministry as prophet, priest, and king, his example serves as a reminder that leaders exist for those who follow, and not vice versa. If we are to lead in both our congregations and our communities as Jesus led in his, we must be willing to set aside our own agendas to speak prophetically the words of truth, to minister compassionately to all, and to administer God's resources wisely. As we do so, those we encounter in our congregations and in our communities will begin to get a sense of our willingness to engage in conversations within and beyond our congregations, our compassion for everyone God calls us to serve, and our capabilities as both church and community leaders.

Chapter 4

Community Needs

Applying Pastoral Skills

Describing the work of the pastor to those outside the ordained ministry is often a challenge. Sooner or later every pastor is asked to interpret his or her role. Whether we are talking to a parishioner, a person on the street, or our own child, the question is the same: "What do you do?" Although some people tease that pastors work only on Sundays (and I suppose that some folks really believe that), the difficulty of the question is not the matter of how much we do. Rather, clergy and other church insiders often use a language that is understood by few to describe tasks known to a small number of other professions. To say that we "minister" doesn't capture the adventure of professional ministry. Certainly some days are monotonous and boring, but even on such days, pastors know that God might reveal a new vision, or that we might be called at any moment to help someone in crisis. Though we may grouse with our buddies in ministry about unrealistic expectations and dysfunctional congregational systems, we also know a deep truth—few professionals are granted both the trust and the opportunity to make a real difference in the lives of so many.

I'm not sure that any week in the life of a pastor can be called typical, but the one I experienced as I wrote this past week was not out of the ordinary. My week included many adventures and a gambit of emotions. Our custodian brought a dead copperhead snake to a staff meeting (he killed it under a nearby house owned by our congregation). That show-and-tell moment produced snake-handling jokes that still continue. A premarital counseling session moved past the typical giddiness of young people in love when the bride-to-be unexpectedly revealed a long-suppressed trauma. A visit to comfort an 82-year-old man facing death (after he broke a hip and contracted pneumonia, his vital organs were shutting down) turned into a time to celebrate a remarkable turnaround as I found him sitting up telling jokes—whereas a visit simply to check in with a 48-year-old husband and father, who we thought was simply anemic, turned into a time for working through shock and grief at the discovery of stage-four lung cancer. I felt like a rubber band being snapped back and forth.

In the midst of trying to help others deal with their emotions (and mine too), our community hospital called a "code black," an emergency requiring all personnel, including a host of volunteer chaplains, to care for over 100 middle-school students suffering from what appeared to be food poisoning. I spent the afternoon helping our hospital staff manage frantic parents and frightened children before rushing back to the church to present a quickly prepared devotional. My work was not over, however, because the nominating committee (the one church members run from in the hallway) still had to meet that evening. It was only Wednesday, and I was exhausted. How I felt, however, did not change the fact that there was still the weekly work of preparing a sermon, writing a newsletter article, and fielding a ton of correspondence, e-mail, and phone calls.

How in the world does a pastor explain all this activity to people who might experience once in a lifetime the kinds of events we deal with every week? Few people understand the work of a pastor, and it can seem as if even fewer care. If others are going to understand and value the work of pastors, however, it is up to pastors to demonstrate our skills, explain our work, and claim our value in our communities. The week I just described offered just such an opportunity as I made time in my busy schedule to attend a chamber of commerce board luncheon, where we discussed efforts ranging from the fall fair to a new initiative designed to draw retirees (and their money) to our community. The topics of discussion, however, were not as important as the opportunity for a pastor both to participate in the larger community and to demonstrate the value of pastoral skills beyond the congregation.

As much as we might want to expand our ministries and demonstrate our skills outside normal ecclesiastical circles, we can feel out of place in community meetings filled with corporate officers, bankers, lawyers, physicians, and politicians. There is often a vast difference between the church world and what our parishioners often remind us is "the real world." The difference between the corporate world and the pastoral world became apparent in one United Way meeting. During a long discussion over a $5,000 budget change, a local executive grew tired of what seemed to him a small matter. To expedite a decision, he mistakenly made a motion to move the "$5 million" from one line item to another.

Those of us who weren't used to talking in millions of dollars, and who knew that our agency had never collected anything close to $5 million, were dumbfounded. As we asked questions, the executive began to chuckle and then explained. At his company, the budgets *always* dealt in millions, so they just lopped off the last three digits. What we read as "$5,000" (a considerable amount for us), he read as "$5 million" (a small amount for him). Standing toe to toe with people who control large amounts of wealth and who exercise great influence can be intimidating. Jesus, however, did not back down from anyone and always knew that his contributions were of ultimate value.

When we lend our leadership in our community, it is counterproductive to compare ourselves to others. It is much more beneficial to accentuate the unique gifts we bring. Pastors have a distinct calling, training, and skill set that cannot be replaced by any other community leader. Certainly, God calls people to numerous vocations, but few others bring with their very presence a reminder of the presence of God. Others have excellent training in a variety of vocations (whether through formal education or the school of hard knocks), but pastors are simply trained to think differently from other professionals, and our unique perspective is vital to our community. Few people have our privilege of studying theology and asking the larger questions of life. In addition, although God has blessed all of God's people with gifts to be used in our families, churches, communities, and occupations, pastors have been given a unique combination of talents needed to shepherd the people of God.

Pastors have a sense of calling, a grounded ethic, the skill to identify and bring out gifts in others, the ability to encourage others, highly developed communication skills, the talent to teach, the ingenuity to organize and manage systems, and the belief that God can transform both people and communities. These same gifts, given for the building up of the congregation, can also be used to build up the community of God's children beyond our church doors.

Sense of Calling

The greatest gift pastors bring to community leadership is a sense of God's calling to serve our neighbor. People outside the church might more easily understand what we mean by "calling" if we speak about purpose, mission, vision, and values. In fact, secular institutions have borrowed some of this terminology from the church and have adapted it for their use. It is ironic that many church-growth models simply reclaim church language from the business world. As others have pointed out, both corporations and congregations are changing their focus from management (doing things right) to leadership (doing the right things). In so doing, both congregations and corporations are focusing on their core values. Because pastors have long dealt with values as a base to determine purpose, mission, and vision, our place in community decision making is increasing in worth.

The way corporations are increasingly addressing what we might think of as traditional spiritual concerns can be seen in how one of the largest employers in my town, Tyson Foods, defines itself. The company's Web site emphasizes core values, purpose, mission, and vision in language that sounds as sacred as it does secular. Tyson Foods defines itself this way:[1]

Our Core Values

We are a company of people engaged in the production of food, seeking to pursue truth and integrity, and committed to creating value for our shareholders, our customers, and our people in the process.

Who we are . . .

- We are a company of people gathered to produce food.
- We strive to be honorable people.
- We strive to be a faith-friendly company.

What we do . . .

- We feed our families, the nation, and the world with trusted food products.
- We serve as stewards of the animals, land, and environment entrusted to us.
- We strive to provide a safe work environment for our Team Members.

How we do it . . .

- We strive to earn consistent and satisfactory profits for our shareholders and to invest in our people, products, and processes.
- We strive to operate with integrity and trust in all we do.
- We strive to honor God and be respectful of each other, our customers, and other stakeholders.

Take away the profit language, and one might think that Tyson was a religious organization. The company statement flatly states that it seeks to honor God, and uses ecclesiastical language (the folks at Tyson are a "people gathered"), as well as other language that might be familiar in our congregations ("respectable," "honorable," and "faith friendly"). The document further speaks of "stewardship" and "integrity"—I like to remind my congregants who work at Tyson of this fact during our annual stewardship campaign. Though one might argue about whether Tyson Foods lives up to these claims, just as we could question our congregations' faithfulness, the language certainly reflects the understanding of Tyson leaders and employees that they have a calling to produce food.

Similar statements of purpose, mission, or vision can be seen in places as diverse as fast-food restaurants, hardware stores, school hallways, town halls, charities, and congregations. Whether the fact that congregations and corporations are using similar language to describe their missions makes you hopeful or skeptical, this shared language and way of thinking about an organization's work gives pastors a place to start when relating to other community organizations. Tyson Food's statement certainly gives pastors leverage when we want Tyson officials to help with hunger needs in our community. In fact, we don't even have to push very hard, as Tyson already gives away tons of food to various charities.

Of course, the fact that churches and businesses seem to speak the same language will not necessarily change the practices of organizations driven by profit. I know an executive in another business that also has a highly religious-sounding vision statement. He tells me, however: "I don't care what it says on the poster. We exist for one reason: to make money!" Realistically, altruism will never be the primary motivator in business decisions. Still, the fact that businesses exist to make money does not preclude them from seeking the welfare of the communities in which they do business. Just as the welfare of a congregation and that of its community are interrelated, so are the welfare of a commercial enterprise and that of its community or communities. This local connection has been challenged by globalism, but the principle of interdependence still holds true. In fact, pastors and other community leaders can help corporations see the importance of improving both the local economy and the world's.

The sharing of language by sacred and secular organizations gives those of us who come from theological communities an opening into other communities. When we spoke different languages, it was difficult for pastors and other community leaders to engage in meaningful dialogue. Language is more than a means of communicating ideas, however. It is a part of culture, and those who share a common culture are more likely to seek a common good.

As the number of terms we share has increased, so have our opportunities for generative dialogue. For example, when business leaders, politicians, and others begin to reflect on values, they might see the merit of having a pastor (who is often seen as the expert in these areas) as a part of their dialogue. Being present at the tables of community leadership gives us openings to share in the discussions when our "theological radar" picks up values terminology.

Sometimes we even have the opportunity to move these discussions toward a consideration of God's values. Similarly, when we hear talk of casting a vision, which is the chief task for any leader, we can ask questions that might lead a businessperson or a politician to consider God's vision for the community. Once community leaders discover that pastors have been dealing effectively with matters of values, vision, and calling for centuries, they might welcome our ideas about these matters. Because we share some language, we don't even have to be overtly religious in our conversations.

Our ability to address the issues of calling (values, purpose, mission, and vision) is a highly valued skill in many circles outside the church. Exploring their callings helps individuals and groups to focus on the actions that best fulfill their missions. Few people, however, are trained to deal with these issues. Though an increasing number of consultants help organizations of all kinds focus on higher productivity, most organizations (civic, corporate, government, or congregational) are too busy doing and maintaining to stop and ask questions about the value of their actions or the impact of their actions on their workers, their families, or the community at large. Pastors, on the other hand, are trained to ask larger questions about the impact of our actions. Though we too fall into the productivity trap, at our better moments we move past questions of action to questions of being. Wayne Oates, one of the founding fathers of the pastoral care movement, made this distinction between pastoral identity and other professional identities. Oates notes:

> You as a pastor are justified by your faith relationship to God in Christ, to yourself, and to your faith community and not by the tasks you perform. Therefore, this is a shift from a task-oriented, work-centered meaning of your existence as a Christian pastor to an identity-centered and *being*-centered integrity.[2]

When a group of community leaders gathers, pastors might be the only ones asking questions of both doing and being. And because what we do flows from who we are, questions of being cut through the busyness of activity to expose our motives. This dual emphasis on both action and motive allows us to participate in the meeting in a different way and thus makes our contributions unique.

It is only when we operate out of a sense of *being*, knowing that we are called to serve the One who simply Is, that we can approach Rabbi Friedman's counsel to be a "non-anxious presence" (though I'm not sure that as humans we can completely achieve that). Because pastors at our best focus as much on *being* as on producing, we are often the most likely persons to ask "why" questions. Why is our community like it is with its strengths and weaknesses? Why is someone at the table pushing so hard for a particular action? Why are we going to do this and not that? Why are we rushing or delaying?

Though these questions might frustrate those who want to focus on action, in the end, asking "why questions" before we act can make us more productive than simply acting out of a sense of anxiety or perceived crisis. Taking a more existential approach to decision making is not the exclusive domain of pastors (certainly others ask why), and we too can get busy and forget to ask the deeper questions, but many pastors do have the ability to explore both cause and action. Having the capability to think more deeply is a useful talent when we remember to employ it in our community leadership.

Practicing Ethics

Whether we like it or not, any time when we are known to be a minister, we bear witness to the presence of God, and for some people we are the very symbol of God's presence. To some this means that our presence speaks a word of judgment. For instance, even though I have a more open view than most Baptist pastors in the South, some people try to hide their drinks when I walk by at social gatherings. To others, our presence demonstrates tacit approval from God (what we would call blessing). It is not uncommon for a pastor to hear something like this at a community gathering: "I'm glad we've got the preacher in on this. It helps to have God on your side!"

These mixed reactions to our presence can be entertaining to watch. For instance, when people find out that I am a pastor, some will apologize: "I hate to say this in front of the pastor" or "I hope that didn't offend you, Pastor" (as if I've never heard certain language and need to be protected from real life). When I hear comments like these, I often reply, "That's OK. I've heard it before, and God was listening even before I came in." Such moments of comic relief not only remind others and us of our humanness, but also provide opportunity for a greater awareness of God's presence. If our presence is interpreted casually as conviction or blessing, how much more so will it be interpreted when we assume a role in community leadership?

Though we might not always wish to carry the mantle of community ethicist (I want people to know me as a person as well as a pastor), how people tend to interpret our role does give us an opportunity to raise questions of ethics and morality. The opportunity for pastors to help groups think through the ethical implications of a decision relates closely to our dual role of providing both comfort and challenge, discussed in chapter 3. When people discover that there is a "man of God" or "woman of God" in a secular meeting, those who are seeking the welfare of the community tend to feel comforted and are grateful for the help. They interpret a pastor's presence as a sign of blessing. On the other hand, those who have ulterior motives, or some other reason to feel guilty, tend to feel challenged and become uncomfortable around a man or woman "of the cloth." Sometimes, especially in areas that retain a vestige of Christendom, a pastor's simple presence at a community gathering can have a positive impact on the outcome.

Of course, other professionals deal with issues of ethics, especially in the academic and medical fields, but most of these people confine their study and practice to specific disciplines. Pastors who become involved in community leadership, however, find an opportunity to discuss the ethical implications of decisions on a broader scale. Whether we are helping a charity weigh the costs and benefits of a new initiative, challenging a business leader to consider matters beyond the bottom line (such as how the decision will affect workers), or encouraging a politician to consider all the ramifications of a tax change, just being present when decisions are made gives us an opportunity to speak a word for God's justice.

Here again, a pastor does not have to appear overreligious to use his or her skills as a trained ethicist. There are many ways to raise questions about consequences and unintended ramifications. In doing so, we follow the example of Jesus, who continually pushed people to think beyond minimum ethical requirements—to think about the deeper ethical concerns of motive.

We may sometimes sense that our skills as theologically oriented ethicists are unwanted, but many community leaders recognize and value these gifts. For instance, Bruce Hamm, who once studied for the priesthood and is now an executive business coach who consults on ethics management in corporations, notes in *The CEO Refresher* how valuable ethics officers can be to business. Such people help to determine corporate values, create ethics and compliance training programs, guide employees in making right decisions, create systems for reporting ethical lapses without fear of retribution, investigate reports of unethical activity, review case disposition or management decisions, report executive management to the board of directors, and create and deliver ethics presentations.[3] If company leaders value the work of trained ethicists enough to retain their services, other leaders might also begin to value the work of a pastor's leadership in community decisions.

Even when other leaders don't immediately recognize the value of thinking about ethics, they can be swayed if they become convinced that ethical behavior is in their best interest. Burton H. Patterson, who has taught business at Texas Christian University and law at Cleveland State University, and who has practiced tax law for more than 40 years, notes, "Experience has shown that in the long term business profits will be greater for businesses that practice good ethical behavior than those which do not."[4]

Certainly this fact was demonstrated by the fall of Enron and WorldCom. In both cases, misconduct by top officials cost the companies millions of dollars, sent them into bankruptcy, made thousands of employees jobless, left hundreds of retirees without promised retirement benefits, and wiped out the profits of thousands of investors. Even healthier corporations have felt the economic pinch from slipping ethical standards. Wal-Mart for instance, recently paid the highest fine on record ($11 million) for taking advantage of undocumented workers. Given the results when businesses break ethical standards, I would argue that practicing ethical behavior is healthier not only for business but also for any organization's long-term health and efficiency.

How we interact with one another (whether on a personal or communal level) sets the stage for future relationships. Though ethical shortcuts might seem to produce short-term benefits for one person or group, they invariably poison the spirit of collaboration needed to reach larger goals for future benefit. Here again, when we bring our skills as biblical ethicists to community leadership, it is not necessary to sound like a biblical prophet to be prophetic. Though "Thus saith the Lord" might work in our pulpits (and I emphasis *might*), it unfortunately doesn't hold much sway in a community setting.

Therefore, if we are to lend our leadership in ethics, we must find ways of speaking the language of the groups in which we find ourselves. Once the group begins to value our input, its members might then begin to ask, "What does God have to say about this?" Even if the group never reaches this point, its respect for a pastoral perspective will rise as its members come to appreciate the value of a pastor's presence in the group.

Equipping

A third skill possessed by many pastors is identifying and bringing out the giftedness of others. We refer to this in ecclesiastical settings as "equipping the saints" (Eph. 4:11-12), but it can be translated into a secular vocabulary as human-resource management. Simply put, many pastors are good at helping others find their place within an organization and helping organizations find the right place for people.

For instance, many church nominating committees save the most difficult recruitment contacts for the pastor to make. Although the committee members might at least unconsciously recognize the power inherent in the pastor's role (a power that clergy must be extremely careful not to abuse), ideally they also recognize our skill in helping match gifts to organizational needs.

A friend of mine once compared the work of a pastor to an old-fashioned switchboard operator. Sometimes we overhear conversations and are able to connect the right people to solve common problems. Whether we are matching a proven lay leader to a difficult task, pointing out the underused potential of an overlooked member, or finding a kind way to move an ineffective worker out of a critical position, we are doing work similar to that of a corporate human-resources manager. The ability to help others to be more effective is a needed skill, whether in a congregation, a corporation, or a local community group.

Our local United Way depends on a host of volunteers to help make decisions about the funding of agencies. The fund-distribution process requires visits to 33 agencies. To accomplish this task, volunteers are divided into teams of five to seven people, with each team visiting four or five agencies. Unfortunately, these teams can easily get overloaded with people who share similar skills and perspectives. Some teams end up with too many folk from care-giving professions. These people are often impressed by the agency's programming but are less concerned with accounting procedures. Other teams end up with several folk who are whizzes at budgeting but don't immediately see the challenges agencies face in working with at-risk populations.

When a committee isn't balanced with people of diverse gifts, it tends to be either too bighearted or too tightfisted with its funding recommendations. When some committees tend to be too openhearted with the funding and others too tightfisted, which committee each organization gets becomes the luck of the draw. Funding, however, should be about fairness and balance, not about luck. Therefore, United Way strives to balance the types of people on each committee. Pastors, who can often "read" people, are helpful in this process.

A respected pastor in our community is a master at identifying the strengths of each volunteer with a few questions. After a short interview with a volunteer, he is able to advise the United Way director how best to balance the committee. He is effective in this task because, as a pastor with the gift of discernment, he possesses the skills needed to appreciate people's diverse gifts. Though pastors themselves, like other leaders, tend to be either people-centered or management-centered, our role helps us develop skills in both arenas.

Therefore, in situations like the United Way funding process, we are able to relate both to those who tend to be overgenerous (out of a sense of compassion for those served) and those who (out of concern for efficiency and financial prudence) believe the agencies receiving funds should work more efficiently and with less income. In fact, one of our United Way workers told me that she often uses pastors on funding committees, because we can sense when a committee is out of balance and help move discussion in the opposite direction.

Encouraging

Not only can pastors serve community groups by helping to match the right people with the right tasks, but we can also motivate people to complete difficult tasks. We do so by using a pastoral gift of encouragement. Secular groups might seek to increase morale, but they tend to focus on the issue as a strategy for completing certain tasks: happy workers are more productive workers. Of course, pastors also depend on others for productive ministry. In fact, most of our workers are volunteers, a situation that increases the need for encouragement. Congregational tasks can be overwhelming and draining, and effective pastors learn early in their ministries to be encouragers.

Pastors, however, probably have less concern for productivity than secular leaders. Pastors encourage out of a sense of calling and a belief that all people are valuable—whether or not they "produce." For instance, many pastors visit a number of homebound people each week. No matter how many visits the pastor makes, most of these folk will not be able to teach a Sunday school class. They are, however, important to the congregation simply because they are a part of it. And because of their predicament, they need encouragement more than most.

Running concurrently with a pastor's desire to be an encourager is our calling to faithfulness. Whereas some leaders tend to focus on bottom-line results, pastors also focus on process and transformational learning. Like Barnabas, we know that a person's failure at one task doesn't indicate that he or she is a failure. We remain faithful to others, even amid their failures, because God is faithful to us, and faithfulness is a powerful motivator. When I was learning to water-ski at age 12, it took me all summer. I kept at it, however, because a faithful adult mentor stayed with me until I got it right. Though it was a hot, boring job to drive the boat around in circles every time I fell, her willingness to stick with me encouraged me to keep trying until I got it.

In both the business and nonprofit worlds, the focus is often on accomplishing specific goals within a limited time (with negative consequences for failing to meet these objectives). In the long run, however, expressing faith in others and reminding people of God's faithfulness to us all is a more powerful motivator than setting productivity goals. A call to faithfulness from a faithful leader often leads people to make a stronger commitment toward meeting the organization's goals, even when the tasks seem insurmountable. Pastors are often able to look beyond the stated goal to see the higher goal of helping people develop through both success and failure. When others might say that a person just doesn't fit in a community organization, a pastor might faithfully work with the volunteer until he or she gains competence in the tasks at hand or finds a suitable niche in another task.

The same skills we use in growing disciples for ministry can be used to grow faithful community volunteers. Many of the issues faced by local communities seem insurmountable and can quickly overwhelm the limited number of concerned citizens. Such issues as economic development, educational support, and quality of life are perpetual concerns that require continual commitment to working together as a community. The seemingly unending challenge of continually rallying and focusing citizens on pressing needs is draining for all leaders.

However, because it is the same task we pastors face within our congregations, we have learned to be encouragers.

Being people of faith proves to be an asset that can be translated to the world outside our congregation. In fact, faithful participation in community leadership can be a powerful witness without being directly church related. For instance, one of the issues that drew me into community leadership was the need for better school facilities. As I related earlier, a letter I wrote to the head of the citizens' group pushing for new schools placed me front and center in this concern. Unfortunately, the original plan for new school construction was defeated for a variety of reasons. What was supposed to be a victory party on the night of the bond referendum began to feel like a wake for our efforts. I too felt defeated, but since we had moved into a pastor's area of expertise (remaining hopeful despite seeming defeat), people started turning to me for comfort. Fortunately, I was not the only person of faith present, and the group decided not to give up.

Over the next few weeks we met several times and began to brainstorm other ways to accomplish the task. Through the faithful and creative leadership of these community leaders, our community found a new plan. Instead of building one new high school, we addressed another need: we built four new middle schools. (We are now, eight years later, looking at high school needs again.)

I learned through these processes that just as individual Christians and entire congregations have to reaffirm their faith when they encounter setbacks, so too do communities. The fact that a congregation experiences difficulty doesn't mean that God doesn't care, nor does it change the congregation's call. Similarly, when a community fails to come together around one plan, it doesn't mean that God is any less concerned for this larger set of people or that we should quit trying. Pastors who answer the call to community leadership and who understand God's faithfulness have the opportunity to motivate others to serve our communities faithfully.

Communicating

In any task, communicating needs and articulating plans is vital. Pastors are trained in these skills and continue to hone them through our weekly tasks of preaching, teaching, and writing. Though it is through pastoral care that we encounter people on the most personal level, offering us opportunities to earn trust and giving us credibility to speak, our most public leadership task is preaching.

As a Baptist, I serve at the pleasure of my congregation and know that strong pastoral care skills are a key to long tenure. As important as I view caring, however, every congregation with which I have ever interviewed has ranked strong pulpit skills as its top priority. Church members might love us for being caring, but their gratitude for one gift doesn't preclude their expecting others. Pastors who do not develop strong communication skills have a difficult time in a local parish, because most congregations depend on the pastor to be the primary communicator of the gospel and the congregation's mission.

Like congregations, community groups also need effective communicators to share their vision and articulate their message. Most major corporations and many municipalities have public relations officers who are the primary spokespeople for their organizations. The best of these tend to be well-paid professionals because large organizations, whether in the public or the private sector, realize the value of effective communication. Often, how we say something is as important as what we say.

Though many of us are tired of hearing more spin than substance in areas such as politics, the fact that politicians depend heavily on message makers reflects the importance they place on communicating their message with precision and power. Though most pastors would cringe at being compared to political spin doctors, we value even more than politicians or professional spokespeople the power of a well-spoken word. Many pastors are as good at communicating difficult truths as their secular counterparts. Each week we are faced with interpreting challenging texts across thousands of years and vast cultural expanses. Though we may not realize it, community organizations (most of which cannot afford well-paid public relations officers) are in great need of our skills as communicators.

For instance, when one of our local charities faced a substantial shortfall in its annual campaign, its leaders faced the challenge of communicating the need to raise more money without sounding ungrateful to those who had already donated. Complicating the situation was the fact that the largest decrease in gifts was due to reduced giving by the biggest corporate donor. The challenge was to explain that because of a wide range of cutbacks in a major corporation, including a significant cut in its donation to our fund, the charity needed others to step up to the plate, while simultaneously expressing gratitude to this corporation, which remained the major source of income.

It was a pastor who came up with the solution. She later said to me, "A light bulb went on in my head. It's a stewardship quandary!" Any pastor who depends on the generosity of donors and who constantly works within limited resources has faced similar situations. Every year pastors work with lay leaders to find ways of challenging more people to be faithful stewards, without offending those who are already faithful. What most of us know, however, is that those who already give faithfully are usually delighted to hear stewardship messages that challenge others to join them in supporting a work in which they believe.

By applying this knowledge of church stewardship to a secular nonprofit, the pastor was able to suggest two helpful actions. First, the leaders of the charity released a statement both expressing gratitude to their givers and offering an honest assessment of the shortfall. (Everyone in the community would be able to read between the lines and know why giving had fallen.) Second, they heightened their goodwill with the corporate donor by allowing the company's public relations officer to read and give input on the press release. The pastor knew that the public relations officer was supportive of the charity and that he was already thinking about how to maintain the good name of the corporation while it was cutting back on charitable support within our community.

In fact, when the charity's director contacted the company spokesperson, he pointed out that, though the corporation's donations were down in our county, its total gifts to charities were up substantially nationwide. If the charity was not careful, communicating the dilemma might anger corporate decision makers and unintentionally harm other charities. Together the pastor, the charity director, and the public relations officer crafted a message that was both gracious and challenging and, though the groups did not make their goal, they went from 60 percent of the goal to 75 percent over the next few weeks. Not only did others in our community increase their gifts, but many officers in the corporation did as well.

In many other situations pastors can lend their communication skills in community leadership. One reason pastors are effective community spokespeople is that they understand that successful communication depends on listening just as intently as one speaks. Many pastors are gifted listeners who can help reframe a person's rambling thoughts into a more coherent whole. Not only can we use these skills in our pastoral counseling to help individuals find meaning, but we can also use them to help groups find meaning amid wide-ranging discussions.

For example, because community groups depend on a variety of volunteers with differing skills, experiences, and values, volunteers often differ over possible solutions or approaches to community concerns, and discussions can easily get bogged down. For instance, a chief financial officer volunteering her time might tend to suggest budget cuts as a standard solution to community groups' issues. Another volunteer, who also happens to be a chief operating officer, might suggest expanding or reorganizing the group's programming. A pastor overhearing this discussion, however, might help these two to hear one another, realize they are working toward the same goals, and work together to reach a better solution than either alone might have devised.

A reflective pastor can aid in finding consensus by rephrasing and reframing statements for various participants. Many pastors know not only how to help groups hear one another but also how to expand conversations, explore solutions that draw on the strengths of several people's ideas, or elicit contributions from quieter (but often more reflective) team members. For instance, one pastor in our local ministerial association is adept at summarizing an entire group's thoughts in a way that leads to new solutions. He is often silent throughout the discussion, but at the end he makes a great statement that sounds something like this: "It sounds like you guys all have some good ideas that lead to our goal. [He then summarizes the ideas.] We seem, however, to be missing each other. Perhaps we can look at it like this. . . ." He then goes on to incorporate the various ideas of the group into a cohesive rationale and action plan. I'm certain that he, as well as numerous other pastors, has developed these communication and action skills by sitting through countless congregational committee meetings. Who knew we were learning a valuable skill?

This ability to listen to others and to articulate the common ground is a highly useful art in working with community groups across various disciplines. For instance, my first assignment in our community's vision group was to bring together educators and business owners to address our worrisome high-school dropout rate. What I soon realized is that educators and business people approach problems in completely different ways. To complicate matters, the more I listened, the more I realized that though these two groups were both speaking English, one might as well have been speaking Spanish and the other German.

The educators were talking about outcomes, and the business folk were talking about productivity. The business folk were concerned about turning out trained workers, and the educators were hoping to graduate thoughtful and adaptive students. The educators didn't have to worry about profits, and the business leaders didn't understand dealing with government structures in which funding and curriculum decisions are made at the state or national level—out of the control of the local educators. Both, however, were highly concerned that half of the young people in our community were dropping out before completing high school—an outcome that met no one's goals.

As a pastor, I was one of the few folk who understood a little of both the educational and business languages. Pastors have to deal with business matters like budgets, supervision, and productivity of our "workforce," but we are in a business that values education. So despite many misunderstandings about why the educators couldn't just run the schools like a business, or why business people couldn't understand the value of learning for learning's sake, I was able to interpret and reinterpret until we found consensus.

What this group discovered through the process was that their problems affected one another greatly (without a healthy business climate there would be no tax base for schools, and without effective educational systems the workforce for business would be substandard). Despite continued misunderstandings, they soon found ways of cooperating to increase the graduation rate by 10 percent over five years. These leaders possessed the knowledge and skills to address our dropout problem; they simply needed someone to help them communicate more clearly with each other. Many pastors employ the skills of listening, interpreting, and clarifying within our congregations; these same skills can be used to strengthen our communities.

Another communication skill that is often a part of a pastor's work is writing. We write newsletters, pastoral letters, and a host of other pieces of correspondence. Writing skills are greatly sought after and respected in many areas. Many organizations struggle to articulate their mission clearly and consistently through various publications. Like our corporate counterparts, pastors also face the task of putting difficult concepts onto the written page. What pastor hasn't been asked to write a letter to the congregation explaining a delicate decision made by the board? Board leaders ask us to do so, sometimes even when we disagreed with the decision, because they trust our ability to communicate complex ideas with clarity and respect. Although we often ask a board chair or other key lay leader to co-sign letters to the congregation, we are often the ones with the strongest skills to draft letters that clearly convey compassion and challenge.

These writing skills can also be valuable in community leadership. For instance, charities need volunteers who are able to write effective brochures or letters to explain the organization's priorities, to solicit funds, or to thank contributors. Civic clubs need writers to help publish informative and challenging pieces for their newsletters. And community advocacy groups look for steering committee members who can write letters or opinion pieces for the local paper. Although newspapers have various submission policies, even large papers are pleased to print letters or essays that speak clearly about challenging community matters. Though some pastors might fear weighing in on controversial issues in such a public forum, positions that are well articulated often earn the respect of critics—even if they still disagree.

More important, letters or opinion pieces that are sensitive to the concerns of various constituents and that outline win-win solutions can build community consensus. In fact, using our communication skills, whether through the spoken or written word, creates a win-win situation for both pastors and our communities. We serve the community by lending a skill, and in the process we expand the place of the pastor in the local community.

Teaching

The teaching skills of both educators and pastors have become highly valued by businesses and nonprofit groups. Most pastors have taught more Sunday school, vacation Bible school, and midweek-service Bible lessons than we can count. As we have struggled to find creative approaches to make old texts come alive to new generations, we have been honing our teaching abilities. What we may not realize, however, is that in the fast pace of the business world, there is a constant need for reeducating today's workforce. People who are able to comprehend and teach new techniques are prized employees.

I know of one educator who did such a good job helping a local corporation with a retraining program that the company created a "school" within the company and made her a vice president in the corporate hierarchy. The educational skills she used to succeed in the business world are similar to the teaching gifts of many pastors. One pastor in our community is often called on by local nonprofits, which like businesses need retraining, to help lead workshops on new skills or techniques. He doesn't approach this work as the sole expert but rather works in partnership with content experts deciding how best to teach volunteers and staff.

Like this pastor, other pastors could easily use their teaching gifts to help a variety of community groups. When I was attending training to help our chamber of commerce expand its base through a recruitment campaign, I kept thinking how easily most pastors could have provided the same information about making "cold calls," communicating the benefits of the organization, and securing a commitment for participation.

Similarly, other community groups are in constant need of people to train their volunteers. Our local Communities in Schools program (a mentoring organization) spends much of its time, energy, and resources training volunteers to work with children and youth. Though this is not my area of expertise, our youth pastor could easily do much of this training effectively. In fact, one of our former youth pastors became involved with our local juvenile crime-prevention task force, which helps distribute federal block grants to various agencies throughout our community. Even though most of our congregation's teens were not "at risk," he was able to use his general knowledge of teen behavior to educate other panel members about which programs were most likely to succeed. By serving on this committee, he did much to raise the level of respect for all pastors and our ability to teach and lead.

Organizing and Managing Systems

When I asked our local lectionary group what pastoral skill most readily translated to community leadership, my friend Matthew Miller, pastor of the Lutheran Church of the Atonement in Wilkesboro, quickly said, "We're not afraid of committees!" Though the organization of our congregations varies greatly, one common thread seems to be committees—groups of people who meet to plan and carry out a task. I agree with whoever first said, "For God so loved the world, that God did not send a committee!" However, despite all their drawbacks, much of the work of both congregations and communities is done through committees.

Whether we call them committees, task forces, boards, councils, or ministry teams, how these groups function (or fail to function) determines to a large extent the success of organizations. In some settings, working with committees might involve management rather than true leadership In fact, much of our consternation with committees results from their tendency to focus on maintenance over vision or to develop tunnel vision about one area of the organization. But at its best, organizing a group to meet a congregation's or community's ministry objectives creatively is a leadership task.

Whether our ecclesiology is hierarchical, connectional, or congregational, all pastors are faced with the task of helping committees to function more healthily. Effective leadership produces results by ensuring that groups clearly identify their task, that people's gifts are matched to ministry, and that workers receive the support and resources they need to accomplish their task. Pastors vary in their style of working with governing boards and other committees, often depending on congregational size. Pastoral-size congregations may have very few committees and an informal decision-making process, and the pastor may attend almost every meeting. Larger congregations, however, may have multiple levels of structure with numerous staff members, and the pastor may meet primarily with key leadership. Whether the pastor is leading through presence, or leading through other leaders, the pastor's role is to lead, or help others to lead, effectively. Both congregational and community groups need leaders who can help structure the organization and manage the system to meet its mission.

As we work with organizations and systems, the work of James M. Kouzes and Barry Z. Posner, who have been researching leadership for 20 years, can be helpful. They note:

> Regardless of level, place, discipline, style, race, age, gender, religion, or personality, leaders exhibit similar behaviors when they guide others along pioneering journeys. . . . We found that when performing their best, leaders

> 1. Model the Way
> 2. Inspire a Shared Vision
> 3. Challenge the Process
> 4. Enable Others to Act
> 5. Encourage the Heart

> The Five Practices are not the private property of the people we studied or the personal domain of a few select, shining stars. . . . Leadership is a process ordinary people

use when they are bringing forth the best from themselves and others. [5]

Many pastors excel at these leadership tasks. As we use our leadership skills, pastors can often help groups focus on their specific assignment while ensuring that every committee works toward the organization's mission. For instance, my friend Paul Hugger serves as chaplain of Wilkes Regional Medical Center and director of the Wilkes Community Health Council. In this dual role, he provides pastoral care to the staff and patients of our 130-bed community hospital while also coordinating the work of 10 community-health task forces (substance abuse prevention, dental health, fitness and nutrition, domestic and sexual violence prevention, healthy mothers and babies, childhood physical fitness, charity-care pharmaceuticals, parish nurse ministry, chronic-disease prevention, and youth violence and suicide prevention). Paul is highly successful in these roles because his experience as a pastor gives him the tools needed to recruit volunteers, organize for results, and motivate workers.

Though pastoral care and health advocacy make for a unique job combination, Paul's theological education, clinical pastoral education (CPE), and congregational experience have enabled him to blend community health concerns creatively with hospital-based pastoral care to create a more holistic approach to ministry. When Paul moved from congregation-based ministry to hospital- and community-based ministry, both his caring skills and his organizational skills proved to be useful tools in leading the 10 task forces to make a difference in our community's quality of life. In fact, Paul often quotes anthropologist Margaret Mead, who said, "Never doubt that a small group of thoughtful, committed citizens can change the world. Indeed, it is the only thing that ever has." Paul has worked across our community to make a difference, but two successes of his stand out—the Wilkes Dental Clinic and the Care Connection Pharmacy.

Dental care became a front-burner issue when our health department pointed out that many children in our community did not have access to dental care. Upon learning about this need, our congregation and others worked with Paul to create a dental-health clinic for children of low-income families. Though some in the dental community predicted that we would not be able to recruit or retain a dentist, Paul believed and helped others to believe that God would provide the right person for the job. Paul gathered those in the dental community who believed in the cause and guided the search process. The group soon found a young dentist who was looking for just such a ministry.

Over the past eight years, this clinic has grown from one dentist working in rented space, with outdated used equipment, to four dentists staffing both a state-of-the-art 13-chair facility and a $300,000 mobile clinic. Though many contributed to the dental clinic's success, Paul was there each step of the way encouraging others, organizing and reorganizing for changing tasks, creatively overcoming obstacles, and finding the talent and financial resources to get the job done. Last year the clinic served over 3,500 people (75 percent of whom were children).

A second success story involving Paul's pastoral leadership is his work with others to expand our Care Connection Pharmacy, where low-income patients receive free or reduced-cost prescriptions. Over the past three years, this program has grown from a part-time operation run out of our hospital's pharmacy to a full-time ministry with its own space. This step was accomplished because Paul worked with a team of community volunteers to ascertain the unmet prescription needs of people in poverty, to research programs by drug companies and other clinics, and to produce a plan and budget to expand our reduced-cost pharmacy. Because of their good work, our community received a substantial grant from the Duke Endowment, as well as hundreds of thousands of dollars worth of donated drugs from major pharmaceutical companies.

When I look at these two success stories, I no longer doubt that a handful of committed folk can make a difference in a community. Paul certainly shows that a pastor's organizational skills can be translated from a congregation to other worthwhile community groups. One of Paul's disappointments is that, unfortunately, few pastors have joined him in lending their leadership to any of the 10 community initiatives he leads.

Transforming

Pastors feel a real sense of accomplishment when we are able to play a small part in God's work of transformation. Many pastors see the discontinuity between our biblical call to living peacefully in community and the reality of community life. This is especially disconcerting to young pastors who dream in seminary of changing the church, only to discover in local congregations that they are now part of the system against which they railed. Perhaps this is one of the reasons that few pastors move beyond congregational leadership into community leadership. If we can't change our own small system, how are we going to change an entire community?

Despite our frustration over failed attempts at change, God can change congregations, and God is at work in our communities. When we focus on God's resources and solutions, rather than on problems and personalities, we have the opportunity to be agents of God's transformation. As church consultant Peter Steinke notes, "Healthy congregations focus on the healing resources, not the disease process."[6] Healthy communities do the same.

Secular leaders who are able to change a group's focus from difficulties to solutions by using the resources at hand are often called catalytic leaders. In chemistry, a catalyst is a substance that, when added to other elements, produces or speeds a reaction. Pastors who succeed in leading congregations through healthy change are prime candidates to become local community catalysts. Before Paul Hugger assumed his positions as hospital chaplain and community health council director, our hospital depended on the members of the Wilkes Ministerial Association to provide pastoral care as volunteer chaplains. When I arrived in town, I was given the rookie job (the one that pastors with seniority avoided) of organizing our call schedule. After much frustration in scheduling volunteers, I soon reached the same conclusion others had before me. The work was too much for a volunteer director to coordinate.

Our ministerial association decided to ask the hospital board to consider hiring a part-time chaplain to provide pastoral care during the week and to coordinate volunteers for the weekend. Again, as the new guy, I was given the task of approaching the hospital board. The evening I presented our requests, another group presented a request for the hospital to hire a part-time director for the community health council to coordinate health promotion in our area. As I listened to discussion of the need for someone to focus and empower numerous task forces dealing with health promotion, I kept thinking, "That's similar to the work a pastor does in leading committees and teams."

I was grateful that the hospital board voted to fund both our part-time chaplain and their part-time health promoter, but I couldn't help thinking that a pastor could do both jobs. It also seemed reasonable that a full-time person would increase the effectiveness of both groups. I shared my ideas with the hospital CEO, and to my surprise, he listened intently. He made a few phone calls to his board and within a week the two part-time positions were merged into one full-time position. The board chair of the community health council and I were recruited to serve with the CEO as the search committee to fill the new position.

As one who deals with slow-moving congregations, I was surprised that any organization could move so quickly and that our hospital would be so open to a suggestion from a parish pastor. I soon discovered, however, that our hospital CEO was a person of faith who valued the work of pastors. Both that CEO and the one who followed have been open to working with pastors and other community leaders in expanding the definition and role of health care in our rural community. Their friendship and openness to pastoral leadership has encouraged me to be bolder in sharing my ideas in other community settings.

As I have stretched myself to move beyond the congregation and into community leadership, I have discovered that leaders appreciate leaders—no matter what our title. The skills pastors employ in our congregations—using our sense of calling; practicing ethics; equipping, encouraging, communicating, teaching, organizing, and transforming organizations—are also skills needed by our communities. Pastors possess more leadership ability than we give ourselves credit for. When we learn to translate our skills, and begin to understand the skills of other leaders, we earn our place at the table of community leadership.

Chapter 5

Getting to It

How to Engage in Community Leadership

To exercise community leadership requires starting where we are and using what opportunities we have to create better communities. There is no "magical model" of community leadership that will work in all places and all times, but we can learn from sharing examples and ideas with one another. It is my hope in sharing my journey that you can translate these experiences and suggestions for your own setting. Even when these ideas do not translate directly to your situation, I hope to spur related ideas to strengthen your role in community leadership.

Devising new methods for pastoral community leadership, or significantly adapting old ones, is an approach similar to that of an entrepreneur. Some of the most interesting people in the world are entrepreneurs who create success where others see little opportunity. Entrepreneurs see problems as possibilities and find assets where others see deficits. I have been able to get to know entrepreneurs because I live in the beautiful foothills of western North Carolina, where an independent and self-reliant spirit, inherited from the early pioneers, continues to thrive in local businesses and community groups. People in my area know how to turn limited resources into more than others can imagine.

Our small rural community has given birth to Lowe's Companies (now a Fortune 50 company), Holly Farms (now a division of Tyson Foods), and Northwestern Bank (a forerunner of First Union/Wachovia). Unfortunately, our success has also been our downfall as these companies have outgrown their hometown and moved their headquarters to larger communities. As distressing as this loss is to our community, I regularly remind our people that our community's strength is not in the companies we gave birth to but in the entrepreneurial spirit that led to their creation. I have every confidence that, given time and leadership, our people will use their talent and tenacity to grow a whole new economic base.

I love to spend time with natural entrepreneurs because they are people of vision. Instead of dwelling on their disappointment with mistakes or failures, they translate disappointment into opportunities for learning and growth. Presented with scant supplies, they do not whine about what they lack but creatively use the few assets at hand. In times of difficulty, entrepreneurs view challenge as opportunity and rise to the occasion.

Such was the case in our community during the Great Depression. Because the only crops that will grow in our area's rocky soil are corn and trees, our people learned to make use of these resources. Those who grew corn either fed it to chickens (creating the base for Holly Farms/Tyson) or turned it into moonshine (producing some fast-getaway drivers, who gave birth to NASCAR). Those who owned timber land harvested the trees and either made furniture (creating an industry for which our area is still famous) or sold lumber (which was in short supply during the post–World War II building boom—a primary reason for the initial growth of Lowe's Companies).

Though the importance of making moonshine might not be a wise sermon illustration, the entrepreneurial spirit of these mountain people is a hopeful example for those who wish to become community entrepreneurs. Using our creativity to make the best use of limited congregational resources is a good practice for pastors, and we can use the same skill to find inroads into community leadership.

Starting Where We Are: Our Resources

What resources do pastors and congregations possess that, if used wisely, can help us strengthen our place in community leadership? What is the seed that, if planted and nurtured, can grow fruit for the community? Fortunately we have more than one resource. First, as I discussed in chapter 1, we have a unique training and experience base not available to any other community leader. Whether or not others realize it, pastors have skills and perspectives no one else can provide to the community. Second, we have some traditional vestige of authority in our position. Third, we have congregations full of talented people who are concerned about their community but often waiting on the leadership and support of their pastor. Fourth, we have the rich resources of our faith, which not only provide assets for community leadership, but also give our leadership true meaning. In this chapter, I explore these last three resources.

Vestiges of Authority and Congregational Networks

Though it is fading, there still exists within most communities a remnant of respect for the position of the pastor. For better or worse, the degree of trust we enjoy depends on the cultural makeup of our area and on the practices of those who preceded us. As one who ministers in the heart of the Bible Belt, I can say that even the most conservative cultures are not always receptive to genuine pastoral leadership.

First, there is not as much "Bible in our belt" as some might imagine. Although there are vestiges of cultural religion, such "faith" is more of a social expectation than a life-giving practice. Despite others' assumptions about a strong Southern religious base, the South is a modern-day "burned-over" area. Like New England after the Great Awakening, the effects of revivalism have run their course, and some people have heard so many preachers that any pastor's words have little impact. Second, rural Southern areas are not as isolated as they once were. Reports of scandal in the clergy affect rural areas as much as they do more urban locales. In fact the impact can be worse. Where there is a high moral expectation of clergy, clergy scandal produces an even greater feeling of betrayal. Such situations become even more exacerbated when the scandal is local, and almost every community has some story to tell about a disreputable preacher.

Despite the failures of some clergy, one can also find in almost every community people who have experienced clergy as positive and helpful. Starting with what we have and where we are requires pastors first to evaluate how people view pastors within our area of service. To make an effective survey we can borrow a model from the business world. When the initiators of prospective businesses look at communities, they do not talk just to the economic-development officer or the chamber president. They conduct independent research. To discover how our communities view pastoral leadership requires reaching beyond our congregations (people who are obviously committed to congregational life and therefore likely hold a higher view of clergy).

Asking a hotel clerk, "What's a good church around here?" or "Do you know a good pastor I can talk to?" can uncover a wealth of information. Realtors (who must answer questions for newcomers) and bankers (who lend money to congregations) also possess a wealth of knowledge about the health of faith groups, though they see themselves as community representatives and might paint an unrealistically bright picture. Educators are also a good resource, in that schools depend on many of the same resources and work with the same constituents as congregations, so they often track community trends. Grocery store clerks, restaurant staff, and convenience store attendants are also useful people to query.

If, however, you want the quickest evaluation of the view of faith groups and clergy, go where the people gather in your community. In my town, that place is Wal-Mart, and the time is Friday night. I have learned more about my community at Wal-Mart than from any of the expensive, census-based community profiles purchased by my congregation. Wal-Mart is more than a store; it represents for many people a recreational activity. It is where the masses mix and people encounter one another outside their usual roles.

It is amazing how quickly one can change a conversation about tires into a barometer of the community's spiritual life. "I need a new set of tires too," you might say to someone looking at tires. Then add, "They guy who sold me my car said a little old lady just drove it to church on Sunday, but I didn't believe him. If a little old lady drove my car only to church, she must have squealed the tires all the way!" Then flip the conversation by adding, "By the way, do you really think anyone still goes to church anymore?"

Get the idea? Believe it or not, you can do the same thing with laundry detergent—just ask someone in the detergent aisle how to remove communion wine stains and see what kind of response you get (especially if the person happens to come from a tradition that is entirely convinced that Jesus would never drink anything stronger than grape juice!).

Such research is far from scientific and will probably uncover a wide spectrum of feelings about clergy and congregations. You can, however, intuitively get a sense of the overall state of respect for the clergy in your community. This will give you a starting point and let you know how much you can rely on positional authority to gain access to leadership. If you wish to get more specific, you can tailor the questions and ask about your own congregation. Asking folks at a coffee shop if they knew your predecessor by name will help define the goodwill, ill will, or apathy toward that pastor, and often by extension, your congregation.

The congregation I serve had a difficult relationship with my immediate predecessor, and this rocky relationship was articulated in the community as well. Fortunately our congregation also had a former pastor who was, for all practical purposes, the "community saint." Dr. Wayland, for whom our fellowship hall is named, was so loved in the community that he received constant invitations to speak at civic clubs and congregations across the theological spectrum. In fact, one local merchant, who was not a member of our congregation, gave Dr. Wayland's family a cabin in the mountains.

If you discover that you are serving in a community that still grants pastors a vestige of authority, you might find it easier to gain access to leadership circles. Even in these situations, however, your access might be limited to more ceremonial roles. If you find that you are serving in a community that affords pastors little formal recognition, you might have to prove yourself as a leader before being accepted into leadership circles. Here again, however, there are routes into leadership other than formal recognition of position, most of which involve earning leadership, and earned leadership is more powerful than positional leadership. Each of us starts with a varied set of expectations based on our community's view of our congregation, its former pastors, and clergy in general, but where we start does not determine where we end.

Even in areas where pastors are not readily viewed as community leaders, there is one place where pastors are always expected to be leaders—in our congregations. Unlike pastors, who spend most of our time attending to congregational matters, our parishioners live in the "real world" (as they sometimes have to remind us when our sermons get too ethereal). Though congregations vary in socioeconomic makeup, people of all stations in life have connections in a variety of organizations and would love for their pastor to share their experiences in those groups. For instance, it was a local dentist and congregational officer, Keith Bentley, who helped our congregation become aware of the unmet dental needs of our community. Largely because of his influence, several people in my congregation and I became involved in helping to start the aforementioned clinic for at-risk children and disadvantaged adults. Dr. Bentley's willingness to use his influence within the community helped me, his pastor, expand my ministry and the reach of our congregation.

Starting Where We Are Welcome

One starting place where clergy are often accepted (if not expected) is charity work. Other nonprofit groups are suffering the same leadership dilemma as congregations and need all the help they can get. As workforces have been downsized and productivity expectations have risen, many people in business and industry have been forced to scale back their volunteer hours. This gap leaves an opening for leadership to those, such as pastors, who have a more flexible work schedule. Although their pay doesn't reflect it, charity leaders are some of the most effective leaders in our communities. These workers have led their organizations continually to do more with less (in business terms, they would be credited with "increasing productivity"). For a charity simply to survive, much less thrive, given the poor economic conditions and volunteer shortages in many communities, excellence in leadership is required. Pastors who seek out and partner with the healthiest charitable organizations will have the opportunity to learn from some of the best leaders in town.

Unfortunately, the decline in volunteers caused by increased work expectations and lower corporate interest in community ventures means that pastors who partner with charities may or may not have the opportunity to network with other community leaders. Even if "more powerful" leaders are not at the table, however, the heads of charities often know the movers and shakers of the community. I am not suggesting that we "use" charities as a stepping-stone; being involved in charitable work for the good of the work is reason enough to participate. I am suggesting, however, that we not limit our community leadership to the arena of social ministry simply because it is the most accessible. Providing effective leadership in charitable organizations benefits the organization and our community, but it can also open up leadership opportunities in other areas of the community. As many have said, "The best way to get another job is to do well the one you have." By being effective leaders in nonprofits, where we are more readily accepted, we are able to expand our networks and to demonstrate our leadership ability.

I learned much about community leadership through involvement in our local United Way. I wasn't seeking to become a community leader. I was simply doing a favor for a parishioner who nominated me to serve on a funds-distribution panel. It was not so much my ability as my availability that brought me to United Way. By serving on its youth-services funding panel, however, I learned more about youth needs and the organizations addressing these needs than I could have learned anywhere else in our community.

As I was granted other United Way leadership opportunities, I discovered that the organization also had much to teach me about family services, health and counseling services, senior services, crisis services, and services to people with disabilities. Because our United Way organization is a team player in the community and because it does not want to duplicate services, it proficiently networks with other community organizations, giving opportunities to those who volunteer to learn from many other agencies. I hope that by "lending my leadership" to our local United Way, I have been helpful. I know that I have gained a wealth of information about the community, including who cares most and who is most effective in that care.

Whether we're talking about United Way, a pastoral counseling center, a soup kitchen, a volunteer hospital-chaplaincy program, a shelter for battered women, a program for new immigrants, a youth baseball program, or many other helping organizations, charities are entities that usually appreciate clergy involvement, are nonthreatening to our congregational ministry, and serve as a proving ground for pastors to demonstrate leadership and to connect with other community leaders.

Although this role may be obvious to some, it was an accidental discovery for me. When I agreed to serve on the United Way funds-distribution panel, I had no idea it would lead me into a vast array of leadership roles in other community groups. All I knew at the outset was that a parishioner asked me to help, I had something to offer, and I might have the opportunity to learn more about my community.

Partnering with Laypeople in Our Congregations

A second access point to community leadership is through members of our congregation who are involved in community leadership. Though the number of people involved in community leadership is decreasing, those who are active in our congregations are more likely than others to be lending their leadership to the wider community. As *Bowling Alone* author Robert Putnam puts it, "Faith communities in which people worship together are arguably the single most important repository of social capital in America. . . . Churches provide an important incubator for civic skills, civic norms, community interest, and civic recruitment. Religiously active men and women learn to give speeches, run meetings, manage disagreements, and bear administrative responsibility."[1] When it comes to community leadership, pastors may be the students needing to learn from the experts in our congregations. Before we lead, we may have to follow.

Fortunately, congregants who are involved in community leadership are usually delighted to have their pastor's participation and support. In fact, we are sometimes drawn into community leadership by the excitement of our congregants. I was first told of the Wilkes Vision 20/20 process by a deacon in our congregation, Jim Moore, who was serving as chair of our chamber of commerce. In fact, the entire process of casting a vision for our community came about because of Jim's leadership. An excellent attorney with a sharp mind, he recognized that the chamber was doing outstanding work in supporting economic development and quality-of-life initiatives in our community. He began to wonder, however, who in our community was looking forward to the next 20 years. When it was discovered that no umbrella group existed to cast a vision for a better community and to coordinate efforts to make it a reality, the chamber formed Wilkes Vision 20/20. I soon got a call from Jim explaining the process and asking me to spread the word that clergy involvement was needed and welcomed. Though the process he described might have been enough to pique my interest, getting a request from a church leader increased the impetus for involvement.

If we truly wish to lead our communities, we need not wait for laypeople to issue an invitation. Pastoral initiative can work as well in community involvement as it does when tracking down a wayward church member. When we begin our ministries with congregations, pastors often strongly take the initiative in getting to know congregants. A natural part of these conversations, and continuing conversations, is to discuss leadership needs in our local communities. Wise pastors know the importance of getting off to a good start in a new congregation by visiting the matriarchs and patriarchs to hear their stories and the story of the congregation. We also know that asking a few good questions of our congregational leaders is a great way to discover expectations, challenges, and opportunities.

Innocent queries like "Who was your favorite pastor? Why?" and "What's the best ministry of our congregation?" and "What do you think is our greatest challenge?" can produce a wealth of information. Similarly, we can expand our knowledge by broadening our questions to include the larger community. "What do you most like—or dislike—about living here?" "What group or person does the most to help our community?" "How do people feel about our major employers in town?" "What do you think is the greatest challenge—or opportunity—facing our community, and how will it affect our congregation?" These are excellent questions to help us gain a broader understanding of our congregation's place in, and its feelings about, its local community.

As we ask larger community questions and listen closely to our congregants' answers, we can sense who in our congregation is most involved in community leadership. General questions about community health and congregational involvement can open doors to learning about the specific community organizations and relational networks in which our congregants are involved. People who are excited about their work in the community will be excited to share this work with their pastor; their enthusiasm can lead to more invitations for involvement than we might be able to accept.

When parishioners trust their pastor, they will risk opening their networks for their pastor to expand his or her leadership opportunities. For instance, the director of our local health department, an active United Methodist laywoman named Beth Lovette, has formed a key working relationship with Alan Rice, our area's United Methodist district superintendent. Rice came to our community with an aggressive vision to form a faith-based community-development corporation (CDC) to address numerous needs, including health-care issues. As a district superintendent, he had many connections in Methodist circles and was able to help the newly formed CDC win a number of grants from the Duke Endowment. What he needed, however, was the knowledge and trust of the local medical community to ensure that the CDC's projects were both pertinent and successful.

Because Lovette and other community leaders were willing to use their influence and leadership capital to help Rice, the CDC has gained the credibility needed to draw local funding and participation in its projects. The CDC sponsors a parish-nurse program in cooperation with our hospital, health department, and local congregations. It has also received the funding needed to begin development of a hundred-bed assisted-living facility. Without the vision of the minister and the connections of the lay member, these great community advancements would not have been possible.

Formal Community Leadership Entrances

Nonprofit organizations and the leadership networks of our parishioners give us backdoor entrances into community leadership, but there are also formalized entrées to leadership in many communities. Like congregations, local communities are in constant need of leadership and often have groups dedicated to leadership recruitment. Some communities have volunteer banks where anyone can list their skills to be called upon when needed. Established community organizations like civic clubs reward current members for enlisting new members, and many have formal recruitment committees. A few civic groups are even set up organizationally to promote diversity in membership—for example, the Rotary Club, which limits membership to a set number of people from each profession, and the Jaycees, which limits membership to people 21 to 39.

One of the most effective ways, however, that communities recruit new leaders is by providing formal leadership programs.

These programs give prospective leaders an opportunity to discover the assets of the community, to network with other community leaders, and to discover where their own gifts are most needed. Formal leadership courses are sponsored by a variety of civic organizations, but most are organized by the local chamber of commerce. No matter the sponsor, the groups' goals are the same—to recruit, train, and empower community leaders.

Our local leadership class is sponsored by our chamber of commerce and simply named "Wilkes Leadership." Nominations are taken every year, but individuals are also encouraged to apply on their own. I went through our chamber's inaugural group in 2000, and it was so eye-opening that I encourage new staff members to enroll as well. Our classes are limited to 12 participants who commit to meet six Fridays over three months. Each session offers learning opportunities both on general leadership skills and opportunities for community leadership. The days blend classroom instruction and field trips throughout the area. Our program starts with a retreat to bond the participants into a team. Subsequent sessions deal with a variety of subjects, including community vision, finance and banking, employment challenges and opportunities, town and county government, infrastructure challenges (electrical, telecommunications, natural gas, roadways, water and sewage), tourism, schools, community college, hospital, health department, social services, criminal justice, charities, art and cultural opportunities, civic clubs, businesses and industries, library, newspapers, and radio stations.

As one already involved in leadership, I thought I knew our community, but I learned more than I could have imagined. We heard from and spoke with over a hundred community leaders—including politicians, civil service workers, local business people, educators, nonprofit directors, members of the press, and others. That experience gave us the opportunity to hear their take on the challenges and opportunities facing our county. We also toured elementary schools, middle schools, high schools, Wilkes Community College, two town halls, Wilkes County Courthouse, a police station, the county jail and the federal prison, Wilkes Regional Medical Center, county and state parks, a waste-water treatment plant, social-services offices, our art gallery, a Habitat for Humanity building site, a vocational workshop for developmentally challenged adults, several charities, and lots of restaurants.

We toured places I didn't even know existed in our community, and I saw a different side of places I thought I knew. When we toured the county jail, our group was locked up for five minutes in a small jail cell—an experience I don't want to repeat. We also visited several factories, where I was reminded how hard it is for some to make a living and how much we need to respect the working poor. Few people get a comprehensive view of all facets of their community, but participation in a leadership program can teach pastors the importance of and need for a larger community vision.

Perhaps the most valuable opportunity offered by the leadership class was the chance to network with other leaders. Pastors, especially those who are solo staff, can feel isolated. Meeting other leaders who have similar struggles and aspirations for a better community expands our resources and increases our support system. My ability to refer parishioners and others to organizations that can better meet a specific need has increased greatly. At the same time, knowing that others in our community share my concerns and will partner with me relieves some of the loneliness and pressure of serving as a pastor. Wilkes Leadership introduced me to a wealth of services that continue to prove valuable resources to my ministry.

More important, the program gave me an extended support system and a sense of belonging in the circles of community leadership. Our class consisted of the CEO of a wood-products plant, a stockbroker, the director of Smart Start (the North Carolina initiative for at-risk preschoolers and other children), a retired chamber of commerce director, the president of our community college, a local telephone company executive, the head librarian, an architect, a power company engineer, our United Way director, a furniture plant manager, the chief financial officer of a mirror factory, the county's economic-development officer, a local business owner, and the head of training at Lowe's companies. I continue to enjoy both their friendship and the opportunity to share in the knowledge of such a diverse group.

No matter how well we think we know our communities, they are more diverse and complicated systems than any one of us will fully comprehend. Leadership groups expand our knowledge by providing a general overview of our communities, but more important, they provide inroads for continued learning and growth. Leadership classes teach us about the needs of our communities, but in addition they connect us to larger resources and networks to address these needs. Leadership classes give pastors the opportunity to demonstrate our leadership skills, but they also help us to grow our skills. Taking a leadership class is an excellent way for a pastor to focus effectively on the most pressing community needs, to join with other leaders to multiply our resources, and to demonstrate the abilities pastors can bring to the circle of community leadership.

Creating New Communities

Some systems are worn beyond any hope that they can be renewed, and many leaders have ideas that cannot be contained in old, stretched-out wineskins. Those of us who are more comfortable in older community systems need to remember that our systems may not be as long-standing as we think. In fact, most community organizations, such as civic clubs, fraternal societies, and unions, came into being at the turn of the 20th century. For instance the Shriners, the American Red Cross, the United Mine Workers, and the Parent-Teacher Association (originally the National Congress of Mothers) all originated just before 1900, while 4-H, Goodwill Industries, Rotary, YMCA, the Boy Scouts of America, the Girl Scouts, Community Chest (later United Way), Kiwanis, Civitan, the Lions Club, the Optimists, and the League of Women Voters were all founded in the first quarter of the twentieth century.

These groups were formed at a time when America was moving from an agrarian to an industrial economy. They reflected the need for community amid change and cooperation in the face of challenge. As we move from an industrial to a service and information economy, we face the same tasks of finding new ways of forming community and cooperating with one another to solve problems beyond an individual's control. Just when we need them most, many of our community structures are in decline or in transition under the pinch of societal change.

Despite our anxiety around crumbling structures, we can take a clue from the founders of these organizations, who instead of pining for an old way of life, created new sources of community. As Putnam puts it:

> For all the difficulties, errors, and misdeeds of the Progressive Era, its leaders and their immediate forebears in the late nineteenth century correctly diagnosed the problem of a social-capital or civic engagement deficit. It might have been tempting in 1890 to say, "Life was much nicer back in the

village. Everybody go back to the farm." They resisted the temptation to reverse the tide, choosing instead the harder but surer path of social innovation.[2]

Putnam urges those of us concerned about declining community involvement today not to look back to the 1950s but to accept a changing culture and to find ways to create new sources of social capital. Again Putnam writes, "We desperately need an era of civic inventiveness to create a renewed set of institutions and channels for a reinvigorated civic life that will fit the way we have come to live."[3]

As leaders of one of the largest pools of community capital—our congregations—pastors have the opportunity both to help guide local communities through transition and to help cast a vision of renewed (or even new) communities. Though each of our communities will develop in different ways, our common goal will be to direct resources toward the greater good. As pastors rise to the challenge of providing leadership in the local community, some will decide to do so within existing structures, others will seek to create new paradigms for community, and still others will operate in both the old and new worlds.

Our involvement in community leadership doesn't have to track the methodologies we use in our congregations ("preserving" or "emerging"). Our foray into community leadership can instead provide us opportunities to experiment with new leadership styles. What we learn from our congregational ministries will aid in our community leadership, and what we learn in our community leadership will aid in our congregational ministries. The abilities to inspire individuals and manage systems, which pastors must learn if they are to thrive in congregational life, are a valuable asset in working with community groups. Similarly, getting involved in the larger community, where societal shifts often precede and shape congregational transitions, can provide a pastor with both an earlier warning about upcoming change and successful (or not-so-successful) models of fulfilling one's mission amid societal shifts.

One approach I have found helpful in leading both my congregation and community during a time of immense transition within both systems has been to take a "both/and" stance. By this approach a leader seeks to sustain and validate older systems (as long as they continue to meet a need at some level), while simultaneously developing new systems to meet arising needs.

Eddie Hammett, congregational consultant, in a presentation titled "Reaching People under Forty, While Keeping People over Sixty," used the term "parallel structure" to describe this both/and approach.[4] Hammett suggests that congregational leaders never take something away from existing ministries to start new ones but rather create new ministries while continuing to support older ones. Hammett points out that though these parallel ministries are designed to reach different groups, ultimately they lead to the same destination. In congregational ministry our destination may be more effective evangelism or expanded care ministries. In our neighborhoods, towns, or other locales the destination is a greater sense of community that increases our ability to raise the quality of life of every citizen.

Pastors who actively engage in community leadership, whatever their approach, have the opportunity to help their local communities steer a course toward the greater good of all. For Christian pastors, this calling stems from a responsibility to love their neighbors as themselves. Many other religions, however, share a similar belief that individual concerns are secondary to community concerns. Even those who profess no faith at all often possess an ethic that leads them to focus beyond themselves. One of my friends in high school, a professed agnostic, was usually the first to challenge those of us who were professed Christians to think beyond our own concerns. Whether it was saving the whales or picking up trash along the roadside, this young woman led the way.

The question is not whether leaders will emerge to guide our communities through transition, create a vision of a new future, and develop the systems to support the vision, but rather who those leaders will be, what vision they will offer, and how the new systems will be implemented. We who are pastors need to be among the leaders who guide our communities—because we are called to do so, as we saw in chapter 3; because we have the required skills, as we saw in chapter 4; and because we have an opening, as seen in this chapter. In the next chapter, I will talk about how this calling, these gifts, and these opportunities can fit into various aspects of pastoral community leadership.

Chapter 6

Moving Outside
Our Comfort Zone

Broadening Pastoral Leadership

Whatever the attitude toward pastors, most local communities face enormous challenges and lack enough leaders to make significant change. Lending our leadership beyond our congregations, however, requires moving into unknown territory. At first, we might feel more like someone who is lost than someone who is a leader. Leaders, however, step forward in times of uncertainty, gather information, scout out the terrain, and point toward the best direction. Healthy leaders, recognizing that they are not the only ones with wisdom, seek out the wisdom of other leaders—especially when the leader is on unfamiliar ground. As we begin to look around at the needs and leadership opportunities in our communities, a wise step is to seek out other leaders and discover their passion. Most people are thrilled when someone takes interest in them and their work and are willing to share their challenges and opportunities.

Educators, economic-development officers, politicians, civil-service workers, chamber of commerce executives, bankers, restaurant managers, business executives, law-enforcement officers, social workers, and health-care workers are just a few of the people who are struggling to make communities better places to live. Networking with those whom we know from our congregation and friendship circles to meet others who are concerned about our communities is a great way of expanding our leadership opportunities. Though we will not be able to lead in every area, being informed in many areas will help us more effectively lead in the areas we choose. In fact, collaboration is one of the key needs with which pastors can help.

Pastors know from congregational experience that people are most united and work best together when they share a common vision. Though not every area has a formal process to promote a shared vision, pastors who engage the larger community often find other visionary leaders who share their dream of creating a place of opportunity for all people. I am fortunate to live in a county that has developed a formal "visioning" process known as Wilkes Vision 20/20. The purpose of Wilkes Vision 20/20 is to coordinate the work of various community leaders and volunteers from different interests, such as education, economic development, government, infrastructure, private-sector leadership, and quality of life (arts and culture, crime and safety, family preservation, health and wellness, and sense of community).

As the current chair of the Vision board, I have found that pastors can make significant contributions to leadership in each of these areas. It is my hope that in reading about the work of our various Vision 20/20 foundations, other pastors might take an interest and find similar opportunities to engage in leadership in their local communities. Although not every community is undertaking a major planning initiative like Wilkes Vision 20/20, most are dealing at some level with the issues we are discussing.

Education

Wilkes will have a comprehensive educational environment that encourages lifelong learning and produces a globally competitive workforce.—Wilkes Vision 20/20

Educational improvement is an area not too far removed from our congregational duties. Many of us have children in local school systems, and most of us have congregants who are educators. These men and women work in an increasingly stressful environment of growing mandates and declining resources. Educators deserve our help and support as they strive to give kids the best opportunity for a brighter future. If you have kids in public schools, an easy starting place is accepting leadership in your local parent-teacher association or organization. Here you will learn firsthand the needs of the educational community. Even if you don't have children of school age, you will find plenty of openings for pastors to be involved in educational leadership.

Your presence might make some educators concerned about the separation of church and state, but administrators soon learn which pastors are operating altruistically and which are seeking an easy opportunity for evangelizing or promoting a sectarian agenda. In some communities, congregations adopt schools and form a partnership to raise needed funds, provide school supplies, and offer tutoring. Even where congregations are not permitted direct partnerships, local mentoring groups like Communities in Schools, Big Brothers/Big Sisters, or YMCA programs are happy to find volunteers. One of my congregants, who volunteers as a Communities in Schools "lunch buddy," recently asked for my support in challenging our congregation to provide six more mentors. I asked him to tell his story of volunteering to the congregation the next Sunday morning, and several people responded to his challenge for our members to help these at-risk students.

Once a pastor gets a sense for the educational needs in his or her community, she or he can move to another level of leadership—educational advocacy. Teachers, administrators, and educational specialists operate on the local level, but the majority of educational policies are set at state and national levels (curriculum, testing, special mandates, and the like). As state and national legislators struggle with funding decisions, educators often lack the lobbying power of other groups. How our schools function, however, has a greater bearing on the future of our communities than most other governmental decisions.

A pastor might choose to support education by showing up at sparsely attended local school board meetings. She might also choose to organize a letter-writing campaign for expanded funding. Or she might choose to work with other citizens for the success of a bond referendum to renovate or build school facilities. Whichever method a pastor chooses, there are educators in his or her community who will be thrilled to have the support.

Like pastors and other leaders of our time, educators are faced with the task of transforming tradition-bound institutions into more effective systems that are capable of adapting to constant change. Pastors and principals who enter into serious dialogue will soon discover that they share the pressures of having to meet the expectations of many constituents, the need to introduce new methods to reluctant participants, and the challenge of doing both with scarce resources.

While pastors attempt to satisfy constituencies that include everyone from preschoolers to senior adults, school superintendents answer to local boards while being measured by national standards (not to mention parents and local businesses). Pastors wanting to initiate change face reluctant boards, wary parishioners, and nervous judicatories. Teachers attempting new methods are challenged by suspicious parents, worried administrators, and those who enforce test-score standards. Similarly, both pastors and educators at all levels are being asked to expand programming while facing reductions in budget and personnel (both volunteers and paid staff). When pastors and educators recognize the squeeze on leaders in all helping professions, we have the opportunity to create alliances in which we can support and learn from one another.

Building relationships with educators has given me an opening to develop key friendships and to glean from my friends which models of leadership have been successful for them. In fact, I have informally adopted the president of Wilkes Community College, Dr. Gordon Burns, as one of my mentors. Gordon brings a rare combination of practicality and innovation to his work at our community college and his service throughout our community. For instance, when a major textile plant in our town closed, he worked with his faculty to create a "mini-semester" during the middle of the school term. This flexibility allowed these workers to begin retraining immediately, taking full advantage of limited monies available from the North American Free Trade Agreement (NAFTA). Because of his ability to str... dollars and find creative solutions, I call upon Gordon when I need advice with my own leadership challenges.

Another retired educator in our congregation demonstrates similar vision. Dr. Conrad Shaw is a key lay leader in my congregation who served as a teacher, elementary school principal, and vice president of our community college. In each position, he made a positive impact upon the systems. For instance, he was one of the first administrators to implement a phonics reading program in our state. Despite positive results in reading test scores, Conrad had to fight the system, which had endorsed a sight-reading curriculum, to maintain his program. It is precisely because of his ingenuity and willingness to challenge a hierarchical structure, however, that he is one of my first "go-to" leaders when I want to attempt change within our congregation.

While educators have much to teach pastors, this relationship by no means runs one way. I know of one pastor who was asked by a parent of a troubled teen to attend a parent-teacher conference with them for support. The pastor quickly saw that both the educators and the parents were seeking the best solution for the student, but the anxiety of the parents and the pressures the bureaucratic process placed on teachers were getting in the way. Though he felt somewhat out of place and therefore hesitant to speak, he quickly saw the stress being created by miscommunication. As a non-anxious third party, he was able to hear and communicate the concerns of both the parents and the educators with a clarity and patience that reduced the stress and helped them to hear one another. Because educators and pastors face similar problems and opportunities, we have a great opportunity to form mutually beneficial partnerships.

Economic Development

Wilkes will have an environment that attracts new businesses and promotes the growth of existing businesses by providing a first class work force and infrastructure.—Wilkes Vision 20/20

Unlike education, an area in which pastors find some overlap in training, economic development is a discipline in which we can feel out of place. In fact, for many pastors, the greed, the dehumanization of workers, and the ecological carelessness of some corporations make partnering with any business feel a little like selling one's soul. Even if we feel that the world of corporate America is more useful as sermon fodder than as an opening for pastoral leadership, the people of our communities depend on economic development to provide employment opportunities and a chance for economic advancement. Whether we like it or not, the economies of our communities and the available financial resources of our congregations run on parallel tracks.

At times, certainly, we need to speak out against economic injustice, but we also need to serve as priest to those who lead and carry out economic activity in our community. Many strong Christians operate within the corporate world and need our support. Some of them may even be members of our churches. Economic issues drive much of what happens in local communities, and we pastors will never exercise genuine leadership until we actively engage those who steer local commerce.

Whether we pastorally support or prophetically challenge business leaders, however, an understanding of how the business world operates is a necessity. Until we are willing to learn the needs of business and to demonstrate as great an understanding of the advantages of capitalism as we do the disadvantages, we will be viewed as naïve by those who operate in the corporate world—our congregants and community members. As one local developer jokingly said to his pastor as the developer stopped by our lunch table to pick up our tab, "We don't want you men of the cloth to be tainted by the filthy lucre of the world, but I don't mind it at all." Though it's nice to get perks, how can pastors be taken seriously as community leaders if we do not have anything to do with matters of finance and commerce?

Because many pastors fail to demonstrate an understanding of the "real" world, business leaders in our congregations often disregard sermons as uninformed, and corporate powers ignore our public pronouncements as irrelevant. If, however, pastors develop peer relationships with business leaders, we gain a better understanding of the challenges our congregants and community members face, as well as develop mutual respect.

Pastors recognize that our work of casting visions, setting goals, and organizing congregations for effectiveness corresponds to similar work of corporate leaders, but unless a businessperson is active in congregational leadership, she or he might not recognize the talents pastors bring to economic-development issues. If, however, a pastor serves side by side with a business executive on a committee to recruit new industry to the community, he or she will have the opportunity to demonstrate that leadership lessons learned within the congregation are also beneficial outside the congregation.

Though she is not a pastor, Christian motivational writer Laurie Beth Jones has translated many lessons learned in congregational life into best-selling books for corporate leaders, including *Jesus, CEO: Using Ancient Wisdom for Visionary Leadership* (Hyperion, 1995); *The Path: Creating Your Mission Statement for Work and Life* (Hyperion, 1996); and *Jesus, Life Coach: Learn from the Best* (Thomas Nelson, 2004). Though Jones's work might seem a bit too pithy for some theologians, its success clearly demonstrates that business leaders are open to learning from people of faith.

If pastors are to earn the respect of corporate leaders, however, we must do more than demonstrate our leadership abilities outside the congregation. We must also demonstrate an understanding of the world in which our congregants and community members live. Secular leaders will not value the contribution of sacred leaders (whether we are being complimentary or critical) until we demonstrate that we value the contributions they make to community life. To show such empathy (a skill we pastors need to exercise) requires an understanding of the challenges and opportunities faced by those whom we seek to serve.

One of my more practical seminary professors advised his students to visit the worksites of our people as a way to gain a deeper appreciation of our congregants' life outside of church. Going on worksite visits has been one of the most exciting aspects of my ministry. I have seen inside the world of a Fortune 50 company, and I've watched hourly workers make gloves. I have learned how rough timber is transformed into finished furniture, and I know the difficulties of convincing hungry kids of the advantages of algebra. I have been in bank vaults and coal mines (both make me claustrophobic). I have looked inside an F-15 fighter jet, and I have smelled the holding tanks at a waste-water treatment plant. And every time I have experienced a congregant's workplace, I have grown closer to that person and have became wiser in my pastoral care and preaching.

As I have sought to understand the work world of my congregants, I have been surprised to discover how closely the needs of business, the needs of congregations, and the needs of communities coincide. As one suspicious of the corporate world, it has taken me a long time to understand that many times what is good for businesses is also good for congregations and communities. For instance, our local Tyson poultry processing plant requires so much water that it shared costs with the town of Wilkesboro to increase the town's water supply. This investment by the corporation increased the water supply for the entire town (including several congregations) while decreasing the entire town's water fees. In fact, because of Tyson, Wilkesboro has one of lowest water rates of any town in North Carolina.

In other communities major corporations have donated computers and other high-tech equipment to local schools to promote a more technically savvy workforce. As corporations look at their communities, many are realizing that productivity increases with the quality of life. Like all other community members, businesses are concerned with good roads, high-quality education, low crime rates, and cultural opportunities for their workers. If you have attended a play or concert recently, it was probably made possible in part by corporate sponsorship. These companies do not sponsor events simply out of the goodness of their hearts; they expect a return (if only in goodwill), but the benefit to the community is the same.

Though we may bemoan the commercialization of much of our world, the support of businesses for community events is often the determining factor in making such events possible. Pastors who earn the respect of corporate decision makers, while staying in touch with community needs, have the opportunity to influence the investment of resources by industries toward the organizations that meet the most pressing community needs in the most effective manner.

A starting place for pastoral leadership in economic development is to broaden our friendships with business leaders in our congregations. Many of these men and women work in high-stress jobs where they don't always receive the encouragement and support they need. Though some may "check their faith at the company door," many of our congregants are hungry to find ways of living out their faith in the "real world."

When I was a teenager, I greatly admired a pastor who volunteered as the chaplain at a local factory. He provided a witness by leading a Bible study during the lunch break, but more important, he provided a ministry of presence by walking through the factory offering simple words of encouragement. Over time, his pastoral presence earned him the respect of everyone from the custodian to the chief executive officer. As an adolescent, I was not aware of whether this pastor used his influence to press for more just business practices. I do know, however, that while other corporations experienced strikes and layoffs, this company seemed to maintain a more content and productive workforce. Whether it was the more caring attitude of the company owners (who valued the presence of a pastor), the results of a pastoral presence, or some other factor that helped make this company more productive I do not know. I do know that, even as a teen, I recognized that a pastor's ministry in the workplace can give him or her leadership opportunities in a local community.

As one of our deacons, Joe Brooks, who is a vice president at Gardner Glass Company, recently said to me, "Corporations, congregations, and communities share many interests, but the greatest need for each is leadership." He went on to say that "without leadership, all organizations are doomed to failure." Joe quickly added, "If, however, a person demonstrates leadership ability, she or he will be welcome in any sector."

Pastors may not understand all there is to know about business plans, finance agreements, and incentive packages, but our leadership strengths are relevant in these fields, and we are capable of learning the language. Local chambers of commerce or other local economic development entities welcome people who show leadership capability. Pastors might at first be pushed toward economic-development issues that deal with quality of life, but when we show leadership in these areas, we are often welcomed into areas not usually associated with our pastoral gifts.

Leadership, however, is leadership; and pastors who work their way into the inner circles of economic-development groups can have an impact in recruiting and retaining high-quality businesses. In fact, because we realize we don't know all there is to know about economic development, we often ask good questions. While politicians and economic recruiters might focus on the number of jobs created per incentive dollar granted to recruit a new company or to entice an existing one to expand, pastors tend to focus on issues other than ROI (return on investment). A pastor might ask questions about the quality of the jobs (base pay, benefits offered, and advancement opportunities).

When communities seek to attract well-paying jobs, for example, the process is similar to the one congregations use to attract new members. In both cases, the temptation of congregational outreach leaders and community economic developers is to focus on the strengths and to hide the weaknesses of the church or area. A better match between the gifts of potential members and the ministry of a congregation, or the potential types of jobs created and the workforce of a community, however, comes from being honest and open about expectations.

Just as some people fit better in certain congregations (people with the gift of service might be attracted to a congregation focused on mission, while people with the gift of evangelism may find their gifts more fully embraced by an evangelical congregation), some companies don't fit in certain communities (the smells of poultry processing are more readily accepted in a rural area where chickens and turkeys are raised, while a medical research facility works best in an area with large hospitals and research universities).

When people of faith join a congregation that does not use their gifts or has a theological perspective different from theirs, they can feel undervalued and may become agitators in the congregational system. When companies locate in communities that can't provide qualified workers for their field, or the company doesn't offer pay commensurate to the cost of living for the area, the company, the employees, and the community leaders become frustrated by unmet expectations. One disgruntled member can drive numerous prospective members away from a congregation, and one dissatisfied company can cast a cloud over a community that keeps other businesses from considering a relocation to the area. Pastors who have learned the lesson (perhaps the hard way) that not all people fit every congregation can help a community seeking to recruit new jobs clarify expectations, speak with transparency about potential problems, and take a realistic approach to benefits.

In today's world, in which congregants and corporations relocate as often as new incentives are offered, a good match in both cases is essential for the health of both congregations and community. A pastor who knows his or her community can contribute greatly to creating a win-win outcome for both the community and the potential employer.

By serving on an economic-development committee or helping to form a community-development corporation (CDC), pastors can use their belief that God is faithful to bring a sense of hope to communities in difficult transitions. As these groups vet potential employers recruited to local communities, pastors can use their knowledge of the needs and resources of their particular area to ensure a good match for both corporation and community. When this happens, employers are more likely to stay (saving the community the cost of constant recruiting, and the company the expense of relocation). This approach, in turn, enables the community to move from concern for mere economic growth to creation of a community with a high quality of life.

For instance, where others saw a dying community, Seth O. Lartey, pastor of the Goler Memorial AME Zion Church in Winston Salem, North Carolina, saw potential for a vibrant community. When the area's major employer, a Brown and Williams (B&W) cigarette factory, closed, many wanted to relocate the congregation to a more affluent vicinity. Lartey, however, resisted the temptation to desert the neighborhood the congregation had served since 1881. Instead, he led the church to invest heavily in the community. The pastor and congregational leaders formed the Goler Depot Street Renaissance Community Development Corporation (CDC), bought the B&W factory, expanded the church's facilities, and began converting the remaining space into a 10-acre residential and commercial campus.

One of the first projects will be renovating some of the space into 80 residential units and galleries for local artists. Lartey's vision includes the addition of a credit union, retail stores, gathering spots for youth and the elderly, a health-care facility, and a day-care center. Through his connection with the Winston-Salem Alliance and the Black Chamber of Commerce, Lartey has already secured investments of $1.2 million for the project. Because a pastor exercised his belief in a community, that community is being redeveloped in a manner consistent with the heritage of a hard-working neighborhood.[1]

Government

Wilkes will have a responsible, representative government that leads our community with vision towards excellence.—Wilkes Vision 20/20

Though some pastors don't mind rushing headlong into politics, others avoid leadership in the governmental arena altogether (fearing such activity will result in the mixing of church and state). A pastor, however, cannot be an effective community leader if she or he totally ignores this powerful segment of community life. When we speak about a pastor's providing leadership in the governmental arena, we mean working not so much with governmental structures as with the people within those structures. Though it is wise to tread with caution into concerns of state, there are many ways a pastor can exercise leadership in community governance without breaching either conscience or constitution. In fact, helping to define healthy ways for government agencies and congregations to cooperate is a great way for a pastor to offer leadership.

Too many pastors and civil-service workers tend to focus on the limitations instead of the opportunities. For instance, the issue of prayer in schools has caused consternation in my community (although I recognize that in some communities, prayer was never part of public-school life). While many are still upset that "prayer was taken out of the schools," others recognize that the government was not the appropriate institution to promote spiritual training. Teachers, principals, superintendents, and school board members who have come under fire from hostile religious groups welcome spiritual leaders who seek win-win solutions to culture wars.[2]

One such occasion for leadership arose in our community when a teacher and principal came under fire from a national right-wing institute. For some reason, a child told her mother that the teacher had made her take down a picture she had drawn of a cross. The mother quickly engaged the services of a local attorney, and the child's story grew to include the assertion that the principal had threatened more severe punishment for the child over the drawing. Ironically, the principal is a committed Christian whose husband is an ordained minister, both of whom are members of my congregation. Unfortunately, in our religiously conservative community, the story spread like wildfire, and our superintendent of schools was forced to deal with a major public-relations crisis that was spread nationwide by the World Wide Web.

The superintendent called me for advice on how to make his points in a way that would help the religious community better understand the school system's position. I helped him reword his points to address better the concerns of our more conservative brothers and sisters. Fortunately, the child soon confessed to making up the story, perhaps for attention, and the teacher and administrator were vindicated. Unfortunately, once an untruth is spread on a Web site, it gains a life of its own, and despite a retraction from the national group, our wonderful Christian educator still receives hate mail to this day.

Pastors who learn how government works can provide a great source of community leadership by helping government agencies and community groups (especially those with religious concerns) understand one another better. For instance, our county government funds a number of nonprofit programs, but with increasing needs and insufficient revenues, these often get cut or squeezed out of the budget, and funding decisions are too often made on the basis of political expediency (that is, which program cuts will cause the least amount of resistance). Pastors can make this system more balanced by helping decision makers identify the most effective programs or by helping charities (which are usually focused on their work) understand the political process.

Pastors can also help government service agencies and nonprofit charities to cooperate in a more effective manner. By getting to know counselors in state-run mental health clinics, case workers in the department of social services, veterans' officers, housing officials, and a host of other bureaucrats administering a large number of government programs, a pastor can often help charities stretch their limited resources by directing people in need to available governmental help. Likewise, a pastor can use his or her relationship with civil workers to understand the limitations of governmental help and to aid the development of nonprofit programs to target holes in the system. In both cases we increase the opportunities for people in need to receive help while saving money for the community by eliminating redundancy of services.

A pastor who understands how government works can sometimes help even those within civil service navigate their own maze of government agencies. Wilkes Vision 20/20 recognized intra-governmental cooperation as an area of improvement for our community. Like many communities, we have a number of governmental bodies that don't always communicate with one another about overlapping concerns. To address this situation we invited all elected officials (town councils, county commissions, the sheriff, board of education members, the district attorney, and their top employees) to join us on an out-of-town retreat. Though it was a bit rough at first, these folks soon began to see that they shared many common concerns and began to move past turf battles toward cooperation.

One major concern was water supply. Each town had issues with its supply, and the county officials, who had previously stayed out of water provisions, began to see that a unified plan was needed. The group decided to work together on a federal grant to build a shared water intake at our local lake. Through the retreat I was fortunate to get to know these key leaders better and was able to use my pastoral-care skills to help them hear one another more clearly. Several times we took a break and our facilitator, our vision director, and I would work with officials whose opinions differed to move them toward consensus.

Government officials, whether elected officeholders or employees, need pastoral care just as much as (if not more than) any other person. Though a pastor must guard her or his prophetic voice, being an encourager to government workers and elected officials can open the door to dialogue over important community issues. Because a pastor is often seen as being apolitical, he or she can sometimes speak to a concern without being seen as partisan. For instance, when our local hospital board got crossways with the town board (which owns the hospital), members of our ministerial association took it upon ourselves to speak quietly to those members of the boards who were a part of our congregations. Together we encouraged these folk to open up dialogue and to move past turf issues to seek the greater good.

Though pastors were not the only ones who had these conversations (other community leaders, including local businesspeople, also spoke up), we as pastors did make an impact. Helping governments to govern more effectively does not require usurping the government's power. It does require a leader who knows how to work with people effectively and to manage organizations—two key pastoral skills.

Infrastructure

Wilkes will have an infrastructure that supports life, growth, and economic development in Wilkes County and serves as a bridge in Wilkes' relationship to surrounding areas.—Wilkes Vision 20/20

Infrastructure (roads, power lines, gas lines, water, and the sort) doesn't sound like an exciting area of leadership, and I do not remember a class in seminary that mentioned any of these. Pastors seem to get involved in questions about infrastructure only when their congregations are directly affected. Many congregations have been made aware of their dependence on electrical service when power outages have turned sanctuaries or educational facilities into cold, dark rooms. Frustrating stories abound of congregations that have experienced the inconveniences of road construction near their church property.

Urban and suburban congregations have also run afoul of zoning or code regulations when deciding to expand their facilities. For example, a church in a suburb of a major city in Minnesota recently built a large addition and an expanded parking lot for its facilities. Local codes, however, allow only a certain percentage of any property to be paved. The church built as large a lot as codes permitted, but it was far from sufficient to handle the increased number of cars as the congregation grew into its new space. As a result, churchgoers park on the road in front of the church. Not exactly the safest practice! The congregation hopes to buy more land, but the expense is too great for a church already heavily mortgaged by the new building. The reality is that infrastructure issues affect our congregations more than we might think, and these issues affect our communities all the more.

How services are provided, where they are provided, and how much they cost are issues that shape a community. The first time I saw a population-density map of our county was an enlightening moment in my community leadership. I never realized how much communities develop along roadways and how the availability of basic utilities increases or hinders housing growth. These basic requirements also determine where grocery stores, restaurants, and shopping centers develop. Industries, which depend on good roads to transport products and which use large amounts of electricity, water, and gas, are greatly concerned about infrastructure issues. And all of these factors influence the price of housing, which is often an issue in economic justice. Since basic infrastructure is a determining factor in how communities develop, the way infrastructure is developed is a concern for every community leader.

Because our theological education gives us little guidance in the area of infrastructure, a pastor can feel like a duck out of water at a meeting to discuss the need for a new water-treatment facility. Believe it or not, my father was once asked to pray at the dedication of a new waste-water treatment plant. I'll never forget his account of how the plant manager drank a glass of the treated water to show how pure it was before it was released into a local river. Though helping dedicate a waste-water treatment plant might seem far from, if not beneath, our liturgical duties, the construction of this facility provided a necessary means for my father's community to grow—and the growth of his community translated in the growth of his congregation. And though we aren't likely to preach on issues of sewage, there seems to be something biblical about taking the waste of life and turning it into potable water. We certainly hope that God can redeem some of the muck we encounter in our ministries. If we fail to deal with the necessity of infrastructure, we fail to engage the real-life needs of our communities.

Since we know so little about infrastructure, perhaps the first step in involvement is education. I first learned of the impact of basic services by taking our chamber of commerce's leadership course—where, like my father, I got to see a waste-water treatment plant firsthand. We also learned how highway projects are prioritized by the state, how deregulation affects power providers and phone companies, how zoning regulations are used for effective growth management, and how all these issues have an impact on the natural environment. I still chuckle when I remember how proudly our local department of transportation officer related the DOT's project of planting ragweed along the interstate highway system to nourish monarch butterflies during migration. You should have seen the "oh no" look on his face when I asked him, "Do you really think attracting butterflies to an interstate full of cars and trucks traveling 70 miles per hour is a good idea?" Leadership programs are both fun and educational, but even where such programs don't exist, or don't address infrastructure issues, a pastor can learn about the importance of infrastructure by interviewing a town or county manager.

Once a pastor has an overview of the importance of infrastructure, he or she can choose to join other community leaders in addressing particular needs. I was pulled into the high-tech side of infrastructure when one of my deacons, Tom Caudill, invited me to serve on our local e-NC advisory committee. E-NC is a grassroots effort to bring Internet accessibility to rural areas of North Carolina. Tom wanted his pastor to serve because he recognized that, though Internet accessibility was being approached as an economic-development issue, it is also an equality issue. Children of families who lack Internet access are being left behind.

I quickly learned that Internet providers, such as our local phone and cable companies, want to provide access to all, but the cost is prohibitive. Getting Internet access from major hubs into homes and schools—what Internet providers call "the last mile"—is the most costly part of wiring a community. Our job was to find ways to offset the cost so that service could be offered in more areas. When I rotated off the committee, we were seeking grants to provide Internet access and computers to rural community centers and volunteer fire departments (a hub of rural life).

Because few people recognize the impact of infrastructure services, there is often a leadership void that might be filled by local pastors and our congregants. Believe me, your wastewater treatment workers don't get many visitors and are thrilled when someone cares. Issues such as planning future roadways, developing affordable or well-built housing, promoting green spaces, ensuring equal access to basic and technical services, developing industrial and business parks, preserving historical areas, and managing growth are items of concern for community leaders and areas where pastors can make a difference.

Private Sector Leadership

Wilkes will have a private sector leadership that works together to save a path of prosperity and growth for the future of Wilkes.— Wilkes Vision 20/20

A vital part of community leadership is helping to recruit, train, and refocus other leaders for community needs. "Private sector leadership" refers to any nongovernmental leader recruited to improve the quality of life of the community. Sources of volunteers include social-service providers, congregations, civic organizations, individual businesses, business associations, and neighborhood groups. All of these organizations provide what sociologist Robert Putnam calls "social capital," but Putnam identifies congregations as the "single most important repository of social capital in America."[3]

Unfortunately this pool of social capital from our congregations is drying up as mainline congregations, which have traditionally encouraged volunteering in the community, experience decline, and evangelical congregations, which tend to focus on internal growth, expand. As Putnam states, "The social capital of evangelicals, however, is invested at home more than in the wider community . . . the fact that evangelical Christianity is rising and mainline Christianity is falling means that religion is less effective now as a foundation for civic engagement and bridging the social gap."[4]

This leadership challenge faced by our communities will return to affect all congregations—whether mainline or evangelical. As community involvement wanes, our neighborhoods and towns suffer. When our fields of ministry suffer, so do our congregations. If mainline congregations follow the lead of evangelical congregations and refocus our members on internal growth, we will harm ourselves in the long run. Similarly, if evangelical pastors don't come to see the need to encourage broader community involvement, their congregations too will suffer.

Effective pastors know how to recruit, train, and nurture leaders within our congregations, and these same skills can be used to help fill community leadership gaps and to encourage current community leaders. As we broaden our leadership within our local communities, we become more attuned to the leadership needs of these community groups. Our increased awareness creates opportunity to lead skilled congregants to share their gifts with the greater community.

For instance, when our local pastoral counseling center advisory board was formed, it had a disproportionate number of pastors. We shared a vision, but unfortunately, we also shared the same basic skill set. As one astute pastor said, "If this center is going to become a successful ministry, we'd better expand our board to include someone who knows how to handle money, someone who knows legal issues, and someone with deeper pockets." We soon recruited a banker, a certified public accountant, two lawyers, and a couple of successful businesspeople to join our board. With their added input, the center is flourishing and continues to expand to this day.

Just as pastors can develop tunnel vision as we focus on our congregations, other private-sector leaders often fail to see the larger community as they attend to their organizations. Pastors, however, have the opportunity to intermingle with a wider cross section of our community. In fact, they come to us every Sunday. Most congregations contain a variety of people—a situation that gives pastors an opportunity to make other leaders aware of larger community concerns, needs, and goals. These leaders, in turn, can educate the people within their professions or organizations to rise to the occasion.

Strong leaders are not intimidated by the strengths of others; rather, they use their gifts to strengthen the gifts of others. Jesus was constantly seeking to train his followers to become leaders. Even when the disciples did not understand Jesus's message, he continued to teach them about the work of the Kingdom. Jesus knew the value of empowering others to leadership, as the disciples would one day carry on the Kingdom's work. A pastor who wishes to lend his or her leadership to a local community can provide a great service by bringing other leaders along. Strengthening the leadership of others in our local communities validates our leadership as we become seen as leaders of leaders.

Quality of Life

Wilkes will be a stimulating, comfortable, open, and enjoyable community that enhances the quality of life for each citizen.—
Wilkes Vision 20/20

Quality of life is a broad category that describes the livability of a community. Do people enjoy living in the community? Is it a good place to raise kids? Are there artistic and cultural opportunities? Is good-quality health care available to all? Is the community safe from crime and violence? Is there a sense of cohesiveness among the people? Each one of these issues affects the overall health of a community, and basic quality-of-life questions affect our congregations as well. When our communities are not safe, enjoyable places to live, our congregations struggle to survive.

The Catholic Diocese of Toledo, Ohio, recently closed or merged 33 parishes because of demographic changes in communities, declining numbers of priests, and financial deficits. Likewise, hundreds of rural congregations have closed as the communities they served waned. Len Eberhart, superintendent of the Dubuque District in the United Methodist Church's Iowa Conference, describes the situation in part of the Midwest: "As communities were being established, it was determined that a farmer could reasonably travel seven miles to town to conduct business after morning chores and still get back in time for evening chores. . . . It seems a similar logic was applied to the establishment of churches."[5] As transportation improved, many of these towns dried up, and their churches closed.

Congregations exist in part to serve communities and not vice versa, but unless they are funded by sources outside the local community, congregations cannot survive in areas that lack adequate resources from which congregants can fund a parish's ministries. The quality of life of the community in which a congregation is located has a direct impact on the quality of ministry a congregation can provide.

Wilkes Vision 20/20 breaks down quality-of-life issues into five areas: arts and culture, crime and safety, family preservation, health and wellness, and sense of community. Each of these areas is wide open to pastoral involvement. In fact, our local hospital chaplain serves as the coordinator who works with the leadership of each subcommittee (as well as chairing the family-preservation group).

Arts and Culture

Faith and the arts have a long history of mutual support. From the first century, Christians have turned to the arts to help express our faith. Whether visual arts, such as stained-glass windows, or performing arts, such as drama or the music of worship, the arts help make our message come alive. On the other hand, Christian congregations have long been supporters of the arts, whether by commissioning a visual artist or by employing a musical artist-in-residence. Pastors can lead our congregations to support local artists directly, or we can lend our leadership to community groups supporting the arts. Our local Episcopal congregation, Saint Paul's, partnered with the Wilkes Art Council to commission world-renowned artist Ben Long to paint a fresco in the church narthex. This beautiful work, capturing the life of the apostle Paul, now draws tourists to our community and guests to this congregation.

Other pastors and congregations have supported the performing arts through partnerships to produce concert series or live theater. One local congregation, North Wilkesboro Presbyterian Church, has allowed our high school drama program, which lacks adequate facilities, to use the church's fellowship hall to hold a dinner theater. The Lutheran Church of the Atonement in Wilkesboro partners with the Wilkes Acoustical Society to offer "An Appalachian Christmas" that features mountain folk instruments. My congregation lends our sanctuary several times a year for concerts by the Wilkes Chamber Singers. In each situation, the congregation and arts community both receive an advantage. My congregation, for instance, has added soloists to our chancel choir as members of the chamber singers have gotten to know our congregation through our sponsorship.

Lending one's leadership to promote art and cultural advancement is an excellent way for a pastor to expand her community involvement, while reaping a benefit for her congregation. I've even jumped into the act when I was given the opportunity to improve my acting skills. When my kids tried out for our little theater's version of *Annie*, I was recruited to play Franklin Delano Roosevelt (fortunately our director decided that FDR might not have been able to sing either, and turned my solo into more of a comedic moment). This experience not only helped me improve my preaching skills (drama exercises are great for preachers), but it also allowed my congregation to experience a playful side of me they don't always see. Playing FDR did a lot to humanize me in the community and to open doors for relationships within my congregation and the community at large. Six years later strangers still ask me, "Weren't you FDR in *Annie*?" Then they often add, "I didn't know pastors could be so much fun."

Crime and Safety

What could be of greater concern for a pastor, who is charged with shepherding a flock, than community safety? Many congregants have had purses stolen from the choir room during worship, and parts of our church's sound system have disappeared in the night. Other congregations serve in dangerous areas where fear of the community keeps prospective members from even visiting. Though pastors might not want to assume the role of protector and adjudicator, we can, like leaders in the Book of Judges, lend our leadership to the efforts of those in criminal justice and law enforcement.

Some congregations, mostly more evangelical, have adopted a law enforcement officer, covenanting to pray daily for his or her safety; have held law enforcement appreciation Sundays; or have provided chaplains for police forces. Other congregations have worked with neighborhood groups to be more of a presence in at-risk neighborhoods. For instance, when a youth gang invaded a Boston funeral service in 1992, shooting up the sanctuary and stabbing a boy nearly to death, a group of concerned pastors and laypeople responded promptly. The Ten Point Coalition they formed has grown into a national movement of churches confronting gang violence in the African American and Latino American communities.[6] Participating congregations commit to the following 10 actions:

1. Adopting youth gangs.
2. Sending mediators and mentors for black and Latino juveniles into the local courts, schools, juvenile detention facilities, and the streets.
3. Commissioning youth workers to do street-level work with drug dealers and gang leaders.
4. Developing concrete and specific economic alternatives to the drug economy.
5. Building linkages between downtown or suburban churches and inner-city churches and ministries.
6. Initiating and supporting neighborhood crime watches.
7. Developing partnerships between churches and community health centers that would, for example, facilitate counseling for families and individuals under stress, offer abstinence-oriented prevention programs for sexually transmitted diseases, or provide substance-abuse prevention and recovery programs.
8. Establishing brotherhoods and sisterhoods as a rational alternative to violent gang life.
9. Establishing rape crisis drop-in centers, services for battered women, and counseling for abusive men.

10. Developing a black and Latino curriculum, with an additional focus on the struggles of women and poor people, as a means of increasing literacy and enhancing self-esteem in young people.[7]

Even in areas where more serious crimes, like gang involvement, are not the case, pastors and congregations are needed in crime and safety efforts. In my community, the bylaws of the Wilkes Juvenile Crime Prevention Council dictate that the council include at least one member of the clergy. After serving on this council for a short while, I realized that a pastor specializing in youth ministry would add more to the council and benefit more from the information being presented. Our youth pastor assumed this position and was able to network with various leaders from at-risk youth programs and to help guide the funding to the most effective programs. Both our congregation and our community benefited from the knowledge learned, partnerships forged, and resources directed.

Family Preservation

Strengthening families is an area for which many pastors and congregations already feel an affinity. Our skills and experiences in this area are needed by community groups also seeking to strengthen families, and our efforts can be multiplied by cooperating with other community groups that share our passion for strong families. For instance, the strategies of Wilkes Vision 20/20 to strengthen families are similar to those of many congregations. Wilkes Vision 20/20 family preservation strategies include teaching parenting skills, reducing the incidence of teenage pregnancy, providing affordable and well-run day care for children, providing day care for handicapped and elderly people, and building facilities such as a new YMCA for families and a senior center. Many denominations provide programs to help at-risk families—such as the Christian Women's Job Corps, a service of the Baptist Women's Missionary Union,[8] which provides support and mentoring for single mothers seeking to re-enter the workforce.

While these strictly faith-based programs are beneficial, partnering with other community groups can expand our efforts. For instance, our community has a wonderful program called the Family Resource Center. It attracts at-risk parents to learn about positive parenting techniques by providing child care while parents take classes toward a high-school diploma. This program, sponsored through both government and private-sector resources, welcomes the involvement of congregations to provide both resources and mentors.

In other instances, congregations have helped community family groups by opening their facilities. For instance, North Wilkesboro Presbyterian Church has hosted parenting classes sponsored by Our House, a child-abuse prevention center. Some of the parents who attended these classes were ordered to do so by the court, and many had never been inside a church. By simply opening its facilities to a community group, this congregation expanded its ministry far beyond its doors. Pastors who wish to expand their leadership by partnering with larger community groups to support families can usually find these groups through the local United Way.

Health and Wellness

Communities cannot survive without basic health care. The connection between body, mind, and spirit is basic to Judeo-Christian theology. As pastors we have taught that the body is the temple of the Holy Spirit, but we have been late in promoting health and wellness. As a Baptist, I grew up knowing that smoking and drinking would kill you, but overeating was encouraged at every covered-dish dinner. Despite our blind spots, some pastors and congregations are making progress in health education. Many larger congregations have added gymnasiums, with a host of fitness programs, and the concept of the parish nurse is gaining in popularity. While congregational wellness programs are to be applauded, our effectiveness can be multiplied by partnering with other community groups to focus on health issues. A virus doesn't care where you live or where you go to church, so public health concerns affect us all.

Pastors and congregations can expand their health ministries by partnering with local and national organizations like the American Red Cross, the American Cancer Society, the American Heart Association, the American Diabetes Association, and many others that often have local chapters. I have already related the story of my congregation's role in helping establish a dental clinic for disadvantaged children, and this model can be copied to address whatever health needs exist in your community. As regular visitors to ill parishioners in hospitals, pastors are well aware of the stresses within our health-care systems. Rising costs and reduced reimbursements are pushing many health-care providers to treat patients more as products than as persons. In response, some hospitals have formed ethics committees, and many are inviting clergy to serve. In our community, Matthew Miller, pastor of the Lutheran Church of the Atonement, sits on our hospital's ethics review board.

Sense of Community

How well one feels connected with a larger community will directly affect one's participation in the larger community. If we are to become community leaders, there must be a community

173

to lead. Unfortunately our sense of community is declining, and many communities are fracturing. Some leaders intuitively sense breakdown of community, while others are faced with the evidence daily. Pastors, charity directors, and educators see the lack of community in the declining number of available volunteers.

The decline in societal involvement, however, affects all aspects of community life. As Putnam notes, "The ebbing of community over the last several decades has been silent and deceptive. . . . Weakened social capital is manifest in the things that have vanished almost unnoticed—neighborhood parties and get-togethers with friends, the unreflective kindness of strangers, the shared pursuit of the public good rather than a solitary quest for private goods."[9] Perceiving a loss in community and diagnosing the underlying societal shifts, though important, is only the first step in restoring or creating new community.

Though I have consistently referred to a geographical area as a local community, I am well aware that for many a sense of place does not translate into a sense of community. It is the work of community leaders, however, to bring those who live together into a greater sense of relationship. Expanding relationships create a sense of community, which in turn provide the social capital to address shared concerns. Persuading differing constituents to defer their own agendas for the greater good, however, is one of the most challenging tasks of community leaders. In my own community, for instance, it is an uphill battle to convince senior adults struggling to live on a fixed income that investing in slightly higher taxes to build more schools is good for them. When one looks, however, at the declining number of workers paying into Social Security to support the growing number of retirees, it makes perfect sense to do all we can to increase the earning potential of the next generation. Yet generational distance is not the only impediment to community.

If pastors are to become community leaders, we will need to sharpen our sociological skills at least enough to be able to diagnose the impediments to community in the places we serve. In my own community, for instance, we have a number of issues that divide us. I have already mentioned generational differences that lead to misunderstandings and conflicting priorities. Another issue in my area is a type of regional tribalism. Our county is extremely large in land mass, but small in population. As a result, small communities have formed in various areas, but they tend to be isolated from the larger community. Instead of relating to a sense of being part of a town or county, people develop a tribalism around a church, a volunteer fire department, or even a school. Though these small communities have limited resources, they ferociously resist efforts at cooperation with other groups to offer greater benefits to all. Issues such as school mergers or changes in a Little League program create a firestorm, with small pockets of the population feeling as though they will lose their sense of identity.

What they often fail to see, though they sense it anxiously, is that their sense of identity is being threatened by even greater forces (such as children not returning to the farm), and they can benefit by partnering with "pocket communities" experiencing similar difficulties. A parallel example might be two struggling congregations that fear loss of identity so much that they would rather die than band together to share resources. Finding ways to allow smaller groups to join efforts without losing their own identity is a challenge for the leaders of my community.

A second challenge to my area's sense of community is diversity of population. Like many communities in the South, we have growing numbers of ethnic minorities. As we continue to struggle with issues of equality and justice for our small but stable African American population, a new minority has emerged—Latino Americans. As in many other areas, the Latino population is now our largest minority, and its rapid growth seems threatening to some. Unfortunately, little is being done to bridge the cultural gap with this growing group to create a shared sense of community. Despite the fact that our Latino population shares many of the same values as rural whites (a strong sense of family, a strong work ethic, and a commitment to faith groups), there is little mixing of the groups. Sadly, the segregation of various ethnic groups is seen most predominantly on Sunday mornings. Despite the efforts of some, most local congregations in my area consist of a homogeneous population that does not cross ethnic, racial, or economic-class barriers.

Despite the failure of many of us to broaden the base of our congregations, pastors can still have a role in developing a larger sense of community. As we continue to struggle with increasing diversity in the pew, we can also expand our leadership to promote an overarching sense of community that highlights our commonality (especially around shared community needs) above our diversity. In fact, changing the culture of our community is a task that must happen concurrently with changing the culture of our congregations—each affects the other. Perhaps pastors, more than any other community leaders, have the ability to enhance an area's sense of community.

First, we have a theological mindset that calls us to be concerned about a broadly defined neighbor. Second, we are often a part of groups (associations, districts, presbyteries, etc.) that organize across regional and ethnic lines. Where other leaders might have little or no opportunity to communicate with those different from themselves, many pastors at least know religious leaders in the various groups. And third, our pastoral skills of listening and interpreting for others give us the ability to act as a bridge between differing groups or regions. Pastors have long worked on promoting community within our congregations and can use our experiences to promote community within our local neighborhoods, towns, and counties.

Congregations are called to be holy communities, but faithfulness to the work God has in mind for us does not mean that we isolate ourselves from the world. We exist within, and are called to serve, a larger community and world. When we provide leadership to the larger community, not only do we fulfill a part of our mission, but our congregations receive a benefit in return as the areas in which we serve are strengthened. By partnering with other community leaders, we are given a chance both to learn from and to affect a larger community.

When we move outside our comfort zone as congregational leaders to promote educational improvement, economic development, governmental efficiency, infrastructure development, private-sector leadership, or improved quality of life, we enhance our leadership skills, broaden our friendships with other leaders, and extend our impact as leaders. And by giving our time and energy to the larger community, we by example enhance the faith development of those within our congregations and strengthen the ministry of the congregation as a whole.

Chapter 7

The Ministry Puzzle

Fitting in Community Leadership

Doing pastoral ministry often feels like putting together a jig-saw puzzle. Each piece fills in a bit of the puzzle and gives us clues to the next bit needed. The problem with our ministry puzzle, however, is that we don't know how the final product will look. To further complicate matters, each book we read or workshop we attend offers us yet another piece to work into our ministry puzzle. We want to assemble an effective ministry, but sometimes it feels as if there are more pieces than we can fit into our picture.

Practicing ministry requires sorting through the plethora of pieces available, finding those that fit into our unique style and place of ministry, and trusting God to reveal a beautiful picture in due time. We begin sorting through and fitting together the edges of our puzzle as we work through our sense of calling. We are given some help with the basic color schemes in the picture as we develop the ability to think theologically. But the practice of ministry is just that—practice. We pick up a puzzle piece and turn it every which way until we decide if it fits into our framework. If it fits, we build upon it. If it doesn't fit, we either discard it, assuming it belongs to a different puzzle, or we keep it to the side in the hope that it might fit later.

Some pastors will look at community leadership and decide that it doesn't fit into their picture of ministry at all. Others will sense that the color scheme is right but that they need to work on another piece of the puzzle right now. And others will find community leadership to be just the piece for which they have been searching. Many who decide that community leadership isn't right for their ministry have a strong sense of the boundaries between the sacred and secular. They rightly point out that you cannot simply take a secular leadership model, splash a little baptismal water on it, and expect it to advance the cause of ministry. If a pastor decides that community leadership lies, at best, outside his or her skills or, at worst, outside the boundaries of pastoral ministry, she or he certainly has the right to hand this responsibility off to others in the community.

Pastors who like the looks of community leadership, but who don't have the time, skills, or support of their congregation, might choose to limit their leadership outside the congregation or defer getting involved in their community until a more opportune time. In my first congregation, which was a new mission congregation, I was too busy putting together a basic ministry structure, training new Christians for ministry, and building a facility to offer much leadership to the outside community. Even now, while I serve a well-established congregation, congregational matters at times must take precedence over community service.

On the other hand, we all have the same amount of time. Successful pastors develop the ability to learn as they go, and most congregations give their pastors considerable latitude to determine the specific shape of their ministry (especially if they see a return for the congregation). Pastors who choose to exercise leadership beyond the congregation recognize that all of God's world is sacred and hope to be agents of redemption.

What these pastors often discover is that community leadership not only provides a piece for their ministry puzzle, but that their ministry in a congregation or other organization also fits into a larger puzzle in their neighborhood, town, or city. As you seek to determine whether community leadership fits into your puzzle of ministry, a number of issues need to be considered.

Facing Time Constraints

The top reason given by most pastors for not extending their leadership beyond the congregation is time. Most of us have filled our days with so many activities that adding community leadership would require giving up something else or blending new activities into old. Despite the jokes we hear about pastors working only one hour a week on Sundays, few pastors find themselves with a lot of free time. We enter ministry to serve God and others, but we soon learn that churches, like all institutions, take all the time, energy, and ability we are willing to give. It is the rare congregant who will say, "Pastor, you're just giving too much of yourself; you need to cut back." A few will say that you're putting too much time into one facet of ministry or another, but they often mean "You're not doing the things that I want done."

If a pastor is to be effective, she or he must find ways to manage time. Unfortunately, most of the places where pastors find openings for community leadership are also in institutions (charities, chambers of commerce, educational systems, and the like) that will also freely take of our time and energy. Even when we take a noninstitutional approach to community involvement, such as a grassroots effort to improve a public park, the time requirements can be extensive. In fact, starting community efforts from scratch can take more time than working within existing structures because you have to create structure as you go. Fitting community leadership into already busy calendars, without sacrificing current ministries or our families, often requires cutting back or streamlining other commitments.

As many know, however, issues of time are actually issues of priorities. As my father often says, "Show me someone's checkbook and calendar, and I'll tell you what that person's priorities truly are." Community leadership must fit well into our ministry priorities, or we will not be able to justify this expenditure of time and energy to ourselves or others. Our congregations, judicatories, and other constituencies have the right to know how our participation in the larger community benefits Kingdom priorities. We hope our exercise of ministry, as well as that of our congregation and denomination, focuses beyond ourselves, but we all fail to live up to what we preach.

This tension between a congregation's call to minister to those outside the congregation and the need to build strong congregational systems (so we have the structure and resources to minister at all) recently showed itself in my congregation. Our conflicting priorities surfaced when we began a review of the usage policies for our facilities (anything that contains the word "facility," "usage," or "policy" is enough to scare any pastor—all three will send most of us screaming). Some congregational leaders wanted to maximize our openness to the community, while others raised concerns about security and expense to the congregation. Like most congregations, we soon formed a special committee, which produced an appropriate compromise (our facilities remained open to nonprofit organizations, but clearer guidelines on scheduling and usage rules were implemented).

For better or worse, congregations often view the staff in much the same way they view the facilities—as an asset of the congregation. Churches, however, seem to have clearer rules on how to share their buildings than they do on how to share their pastors. Unless there is clear agreement on expectations, a pastor who begins to spend time outside the congregation can run into the same type of conflicts associated with sharing the building. Unfortunately, the tensions around expectations of a pastor's duties are much more personal. The tension between the church's call to minister in the world and the need to equip and support Christians so they can minister in the world requires constant attention and clarifications. How a congregation uses its limited resources, including its ministerial staff, reveals that congregation's priorities.

Managing Expectations

Closely tied to issues of time and priorities are congregational concerns about a pastor's role. People expect pastors to point the way in church settings, but when we exercise leadership outside the congregation, our function can become confusing for ourselves and others. For instance, when I recently spoke at a gathering of our community health foundation, I was quoted in our local paper. Though the paper identified me as the pastor of First Baptist Church, readers had a right to ask whether I was speaking as a representative of the congregation, another community organization (Wilkes Vision 20/20, the chamber of commerce, or the pastoral counseling center, which receives grants from the health foundation), or simply as a private citizen. The answer was a very ambiguous "Yes!" When we begin to involve ourselves in numerous organizations, we often wear many hats, and which hat we are wearing may be unclear to our congregation, to our community, or even to ourselves.

Issues of role confusion can be addressed by thinking through which group we represent at any given time and stating clearly for whom we are speaking. The problem comes, however, when we aren't clear about whom we represent, we don't state which hat we are wearing, or we find ourselves dealing with a conflict of interest. On occasion, the groups I serve compete for funds or run into turf battles in certain programs. Although such a situation can be an opportunity to exert leadership by facilitating communication between the two groups or helping craft a compromise, there is also the risk of being caught in the middle and losing the trust of both groups.

Role confusion becomes especially dangerous for pastors when we get caught between congregational expectations and community needs. For instance, it was difficult for me to remain objective during the debate about the policy for use of our facilities. I knew that my primary interest had to be the welfare of our local congregation, but I also serve on the boards of some of the groups that wanted to use our fellowship hall for meetings. (In fact, I had invited many of them to do so.) Because I didn't see a conflict between our congregation's mission statement and the use of our buildings by these groups, I had to be careful not to become defensive when I heard the concerns of some of my members about the cost to our congregation and potential damage to our buildings.

Equal to the risk of being caught between the congregation and an outside community group is the risk of getting caught up in a controversy involving an outside group. When you expand your leadership, you accept both the rewards of being associated with the positive aspects of the organization and the hazards of every organization's potential to fail in one or more areas. Whether we intend it or not, a pastor's participation in a group is often seen as a blessing or endorsement, and this perception can get us into trouble.

A denominational representative graciously accepted the position of treasurer for a crisis ministry center, only to discover that the agency had, at best, poor accounting procedures and, at worst, a case of embezzlement. As a person of integrity, she brought the matter before the board. The board members split into camps over whether a problem existed and, if so, what to do about it. The situation soon became known in the community, where people complicated the matter with various interpretations of the story. Despite her honesty and appropriate response, the minister soon resigned the position in an effort to remove her denomination's name from the controversy. Unfortunately, she continues, even years later, to draw criticism from both sides.

Though the minister who became treasurer for a community group fell into a controversy not of her making, a pastor who assumes community leadership can also step into controversy intentionally. Although I am proud of my role and that of other pastors in helping to build new middle schools in our community, the campaign to do so was not without cost. Most of my congregants are very pro-education, but others of them are more concerned about tax burdens than educational improvement. By taking an active role in this campaign, the other pastors and I raised the ire of some we serve.

In a similar fashion, my involvement in Wilkes Vision 20/20 has at times created a misperception in my congregation and the community. Though Wilkes Vision 20/20 does not endorse political candidates, our vision statement so clearly articulates a plan for our community that it often has been used by local politicians—both for and against change. In fact, when one local politician used much of the vision document in his platform, some assumed that I had helped structure his campaign and wondered if I was becoming too enmeshed in politics.

Even when no personality is involved, taking a stand in community affairs can be seen as being political. For instance, our community is engaged in a controversy over the potential expansion of a rock quarry. Some see it as an opportunity for economic development, and others are highly concerned about the environmental impact. Several of the organizations in which I participate have been asked to take a side or to help find a compromise solution. Though we might be of help in finding a win-win solution (such as using the area for a park that brings in tourism dollars, while preserving the environment), most of the agencies on which I serve are worried about getting caught in the middle of a situation in which tempers are running high. Pastors who take leadership roles in community groups run the risk of becoming tied up in community controversies that can in turn damage their ministries and the reputation of their congregations.

As in any worthy adventure, the risks are many, but the potential for doing good is high. Limitations of time and energy are real. Ministerial expectations of our congregations don't go away just because we become involved in our community. And our community might be hesitant to accept our help—wondering who we are and why we showed up. Despite these obstacles, however, we reap some real advantages by expanding our ministry to include community leadership.

Fitting the Pieces Together

A pastor who sows his or her energy in community leadership often discovers that the work returns a harvest of benefits to the congregation, community, and pastor. We do not give, one would hope, so that we might get in return, but neither do we invest our limited time and energy unless we feel it will increase our effectiveness in ministry. For instance, in my community a local radio station recently began publishing a local-events magazine in an effort to increase advertising revenue. What caught my attention was the title—"What's in It for Me?" Asking, "What's in it for me?" sounds a bit selfish, but asking, "What's in it for the Kingdom?" is a pretty good question. If we engage in community leadership during work hours, our congregants have a right to know how our participation in outside groups will benefit the ministry of our church. Likewise, we need to be able to justify to ourselves how lending our leadership to endeavors outside ecclesiastical circles fits into our own definition of ministry. Here are a few of the benefits to my congregation and ministry I have found through participating in community leadership.

A Sense of Connection

When we talk about benefits to our congregation and ministry, we need to be able to explain our motivations to those with whom we seek to partner. Community groups are often glad to have our help, but some are suspicious that we are seeking to proselytize through their organizations. We need to be open about how our faith motivates us to serve, but we also need to explain in nonreligious language our desire to serve. Since our goal is to serve the community, using language about community is a great way to introduce ourselves.

Most people understand a basic need to be connected to others and to the place where we live. Jesus talked about the importance of being a good neighbor, and hospitality is a deeply rooted Judeo-Christian value. When we honestly express our need to be in relationship with our neighbors, we are often met with understanding and welcome. Taking the stance, "I'm here to listen and learn as much as I'm here to give and teach," opens more doors to community participation than "I've got something you need." In other words, if we want to practice community leadership, we have to practice community.

If we want to justify community service to our congregations and ourselves, we need look no further than the parable of the Good Samaritan. Involving ourselves in the needs of the community beyond the doors of our church shows we understand that our neighbors include many unlike ourselves and unlike those in our congregation. When we demonstrate a willingness both to see and to attend to hurts beyond our congregation, we open the door to new relationships. Like the Samaritan, we too will have to risk going down into ditches where those who wish to harm others may be lurking, and to risk reaching out to those who are not like us.

Though the implication of the parable is clear—that we are to love everyone—many aspects of the story are left unwritten. Did the Samaritan and the man who fell to robbers (assuming he was a Jew) establish a relationship that broke religious and class barriers? Or did the one who was hurt feel embarrassed, pay the Samaritan back for his help, and go his own way? Though many pastors and congregations are good at offering crisis ministry within the larger community, loving our neighbor involves more than being there in a crisis; it requires building community every day of our lives.

The greatest benefit I have received from expanding my ministry to include community leadership is the opportunity to meet others. Whether other community leaders have become good friends or simply acquaintances, these relationships have helped me to grow. Despite our working with people, many pastors have a profound sense of isolation. Though I enjoy many close relationships within my congregation, the roles we play as pastor and congregant are always part of the equation.

Sometimes the limitations imposed by our roles feel like a burden—even when members do not intend to burden me. For instance, when I recently took an extended vacation, I decided to worship at another congregation in town. Although I love my congregation, I knew that it would be difficult for me to be present in worship without being the pastor. My concerns were validated when I went out to lunch after worship and saw many of my congregants. I love these people and I was glad to see them, but within five minutes I heard reports on two committee meetings and a concern about our sound system. Perhaps they were saying, "Things are going OK without you" or "We miss and need you," but I heard, "Work is calling."

Sometimes, it is refreshing to step out of my pastoral role, and when I'm in community meetings, I'm like my church members—a volunteer. I can choose what I want to do and with whom I'd like to work. Even when community folk ask me for advice about their congregations, it doesn't seem like pressure. In fact, it often helps me to know that my congregation and I share many of the same struggles as other congregations and their leaders.

Any time we expand our relationships, we cut into the sense of isolation common to all human beings. When we relate to those outside our congregation, unless we have a very diverse church, we have the added advantage of experiencing a wider diversity of friendships. For instance, the sister congregation I mentioned visiting on my stay-at-home vacation is an African American congregation (unfortunately, most congregations in my community are segregated). Though I could have visited other African American congregations whose pastors I know professionally, I didn't just want an African American worship experience. I wanted to worship with a friend, so I went to Parks Grove Baptist Church and sat with my friend Luther Parks. Had it not been for the fact that Luther and I went through leadership training together at the local chamber of commerce, we might not have had the opportunity to meet and form a lasting friendship.

Similarly, a former community friend (he recently moved) is a practicing Buddhist. We became friends when Lance was the plaintiff in a lawsuit challenging a display of the Ten Commandments in a government building. Because of his stand, Lance was harassed by many conservative Christians in town. He was verbally abused, he received hate mail on a regular basis, and his prayer garden was vandalized. When I thanked him for his stand to keep the government from establishing a religion (even mine), he was surprised and delighted. We soon entered into a number of theological discussions, and because Lance questions everything, I soon sharpened my skills in Christian apologetics.

We can often be more open with friends from our community than we can with the congregants we serve, or even with other pastors—with whom we may feel a sense of rivalry. When I was going through a difficult time, a local business manager who serves with me in Wilkes Vision 20/20 intuited my distress and offered to help. When we began to talk, I discovered that a person I knew only as a businesswoman was also a former pastor's wife. Her first husband had died several years earlier, but she still understood the pressures pastors face. Her ability to understand my situation without having a direct connection to the problem was most beneficial.

I relate weekly to farmers, bankers, educators, politicians, and many more people who share their experiences with me and allow me to share my experiences with them. Being involved in the wider community gives pastors an opportunity to broaden their own community.

A Synergy of Resources

Expanding our relationships to include those in the larger community doesn't benefit only the pastor; it also benefits the congregation he or she serves. Like pastors, congregations can also become isolated in their ministries. Even the most ecumenical congregations tend to rely upon denominations or other faith-based resources for programming needs or solutions to ministry challenges. Likewise, congregations that define themselves as nondenominational community churches tend to associate and exchange ideas with similar congregations. The problem with many of these church resources is that they are still one-size-fits-all church resources.

Though some faith groups are tailoring programs to each congregation, a pastor who understands the way his or her community works can be even more effective in translating congregational ministries to the congregation's unique setting. In fact, pastors and congregations that actively participate in the community around them often discover new non-church based ideas and resources that are working for other entities in their community. When members of our congregations follow our lead in getting more involved in the community, they too begin to develop an eye for what works well in their setting.

When I had the privilege of chairing the needs-assessment committee of our United Way, the experience helped my congregation and me to tailor our benevolence ministry to focus on areas where we could make the biggest difference. It was a learning experience for me because, though I was the chair, the members were the experts. Each person in the group worked directly with some area of need in our community and shared with the whole group a synopsis of the work in his or her field.

As I heard each report, I realized that much of the energy I was expending to address ministry needs could have been conserved by making referrals to organizations already effectively addressing these needs. Because I was new in the community and had spent most of my time getting to know my congregants, I wasn't even aware of the existence of many of these excellent community resources. After several months of listening to these reports, however, I gained an understanding of both the most pressing needs of our community and of the people most effectively solving the problems. The report generated by the needs-assessment committee became a tool for setting our United Way funding priorities, but it was also made available to all the helping organizations in our communities, including the faith communities. Congregations that took advantage of this resource had at their fingertips a guide to more than 60 helping organizations.

Several congregations in my area use the United Way Needs Assessment to increase the effectiveness of their benevolence work. Matt Miller, pastor of the Lutheran Church of the Atonement in Wilkesboro, followed me as chair of this committee and used his findings to direct his congregation's benevolence funds as well matching funds from Thrivent Financial for Lutherans (a financial-services company that donates millions of dollars a year to efforts supported by Lutherans to meet local community needs).

Matt learned from his participation in United Way that the needs of many senior adults in our community were not being met, and he shared this information with his congregation and officials of Thrivent. The congregation explored the issue further and decided that one of the most pressing needs was to provide a hot meal on weekends for seniors who were served by a weekday "meals on wheels" program. They sold barbecued chicken plates to raise several hundred dollars; the amount was matched by Thrivent, and the funds helped another charity, Samaritan's Kitchen, provide weekend meals for these seniors. Matt says that the research he participated in through United Way helped him demonstrate a compelling need that motivated his congregation and Thrivent to share their resources while maximizing their effectiveness. Becoming active in community leadership can help a pastor and congregation make a greater impact using the congregation's limited time, talents, and financial resources.

Sources of Inspiration

Closely associated with finding a sense of community and effectively helping our community is the issue of motivation. Though we pastors hope our leadership in the community is encouraging and helpful, we often find that we are inspired as much as we inspire. Like all pastors, I am continually on the lookout for ways to illustrate biblical truths through contemporary examples. I have heard from more than one source that we pastors have a problem demonstrating how our grand thoughts can be put into daily practice. An honest congregant once said to me, "Mother Teresa is a great example, but when you use her, Billy Graham, or some of those other extraordinary saints, you set the bar higher than I can jump right now." In other words, "Can't you talk about someone to whom I can relate?"

As I move around our community, I see people who are an inspiration to me, and with their permission I share their example with others. Though most of them humbly say that their stories aren't all that different from anyone else's, it is precisely their courage amid everyday life that inspires. You have to be careful about using personal stories, because some individuals become wary that they might end up in a sermon if they hang around you. But most people enjoy hearing positive stories about their friends, neighbors, and even themselves. In fact, I've had folk come up to me at meetings and say something like, "I hear Tom made it into your sermon. When do I get a mention?"

The relationships we form when we expand our community involvement encourage us even when they aren't sermon fodder. Like all people, pastors need inspiration, and we don't always get it within the confines of the congregation. Though we may discover greater needs as we move into larger circles, we also discover many people rising to the challenge of addressing these needs.

Pat Day, a woman who serves on our health foundation (and happens to be a deacon in my congregation), inspired me when she took a bad experience for herself and turned it into a positive for others. Several years ago, Pat was rushed to our local hospital with congestive heart failure. She needed to be airlifted to a larger hospital, but our hospital didn't have a landing pad for an emergency helicopter. Like many other patients, she was loaded into an ambulance and driven to a nearby field large enough to accommodate a medevac helicopter. Pat realized quickly that this process not only added the expense of an ambulance ride, but it also put critical patients at a greater risk during transportation.

When her health improved, Pat led the health foundation to raise funds for a landing pad and persuaded both Wilkes Regional Medical Center (our hospital) and Wake Forest University Medical Center (the hospital in Winston-Salem to which she was transferred) to support the project. Today our hospital has one of the most advanced helicopter pads in the state (It even has heaters in the concrete to melt ice in the winter.). Stories like this happen in every community, and they inspire laypeople and pastors alike.

One of my favorite stories involves Beth Lovette, director of the Wilkes County Health Department. The fact that Beth's husband is a chicken farmer puts her in a quandary, because Beth knows the environmental risk of the long-standing agricultural practice of using chicken litter as fertilizer on fields throughout our region. The farmers needed to get rid of chicken litter, and it makes great fertilizer. But it also runs off into streams, creating environmental hazards. People say, "If life gives you lemons, make lemonade," but what do you do when life gives you chicken litter? Beth has been saying for years that our county needs to address this problem, but no one seemed to have a positive solution. Beth, however, kept asking the questions and looking for answers.

One day, at a Vision 20/20 meeting to discuss economic development, our economic development director announced that he and Beth might have found an answer to the chicken-litter dilemma. A company in another state had developed a technology to burn chicken litter to produce power, and they were investigating the possibility of building a plant in our area. I said to the group, "If our community can find a way to make power out of chicken shit, I believe we can do about anything." Though I shocked several in the group with my vernacular, most thought it was funny that a pastor would make such an observation.

My response was only in part about the environmental issue our community faced. It was also about a profound theological truth: when we find God's power amid our personal, congregational, or community predicaments, we receive the strength to go on. A pastor who takes the time not only to live in a community but also to work actively with others in addressing the community's problems will discover that pastors find more help than they give, for a group is always stronger than an individual.

Leadership Development

When dealing with my congregation or with my personal relationships, I often take on too much responsibility and place too much pressure on myself. Though stakes are often high and issues in our communities can overwhelm us as well, dealing with the larger public is often less threatening than facing issues in our congregations or in our personal lives. The larger dynamic and less personal setting can also remind us of our limitations. We can make a difference by sharing our leadership in our communities, but the scope of the system also keeps our egos in check. It is simply harder to play God in a larger setting, so we are less tempted to do so.

Recognizing our limitations within the larger settings of society is not a hindrance but rather an opportunity. Although we do not enter community leadership to practice our skills on unsuspecting subjects, stepping up to leadership in a different setting gives us the chance to hone our leadership skills in a personally less threatening environment. It can be equally difficult for me to hear encouragement or correction, but I am more open to both when they come from sources outside my congregation. It is far less threatening to hear advice from a local banker, who neither holds my account nor attends the church I serve, than it is to hear the same advice from a member of my diaconate. In fact, because those outside my congregation are sometimes in a better position to comment and I am less likely to take offense, I often seek out their advice.

For instance, after chairing a particular United Way meeting, I left with a sense that something didn't go quite right. I sought out a former United Way officer who had attended the meeting. I shared my discomfort and asked for his thoughts. He gently pointed out that I had run too quickly through some of the ideas brought up by others, in deference to my own solution. Though his response was hard to hear, because it came from someone outside my congregation it seemed less of a threat to my professional life or personal well-being. Likewise, the kudos I received from the group, when I confessed my mistake to the committee and reopened the discussion to include more ideas, were easier to accept than those I receive from people who have a more personal stake in my ministry.

Putting ourselves in a less threatening environment where we pastors can receive correction and affirmation is not the only benefit of practicing leadership in the larger community. Expanding the circles in which we operate increases our contact with other leaders, and this experience increases our opportunities to learn.

While most pastors are fortunate to have a variety of leaders within our congregations, an even larger pool of leaders from whom we can learn is available in our community. Even though these leaders serve a variety of interests, good leaders recognize that most leadership skills translate to a host of settings. A CEO who understands that a sense of purpose is a more powerful motivator than remuneration can remind a pastor that although we can't offer our congregants pay, we can offer them an opportunity to make a difference. So we follow the CEO's lead, or perhaps she follows ours, in transforming our organizations from committees, which tend to make decisions (many of which seem trivial), to self-directed work groups, which tend to take more ownership and action.

We might learn from the head of a nonprofit group, who like us works mainly with volunteers, how matching people's skills to organizational need keeps the volunteer happier and accomplishes the needed task. So we come to see how a gifts-based approach, which we knew was more biblically accurate, can increase the effectiveness of any organization. Whether we learn something new or we are shown how something we already know can be better implemented, the simple experience of sharing with other community leaders is beneficial.

New Members

Although all the benefits of providing community leadership have a positive though indirect impact on our congregation by strengthening the key congregational leader, most congregations will want evidence of a direct impact before they lend their leader to the larger community. Though this view may be a reflection of my Baptist roots, the overabundance of church growth material developed in the past several decades leads me to believe that the benefit most congregations seek is numerical growth. Whether this goal comes from a desire to make disciples or from a need to get workers to serve the institution, the question is the same—"Will our pastor's participation in the larger community get us new members?"

Although this book is clearly not intended as a church growth manual and my primary motivation for engaging in community leadership is not primarily church outreach (to be honest, it was probably a need for diversity in my ministry), there is a payoff when we expand our circles of influence. As we minister within our congregations, an unintended consequence can often be that we become isolated from anyone outside the church we serve. How can we reach the nonchurched if we only minister among the churched?

As I have expanded my involvement in the larger community, I have gained the opportunity to make friends with many people who have lost interest in, or never had an interest in, congregational life. Though I enjoy leading in a nonchurch setting, expanding my participation in the larger community also increases my opportunity for pastoral ministry. Sometimes the opportunity comes because others know I am a pastor, and sometimes because they don't. Unfortunately many people who choose not to involve themselves within a congregation do so because of a negative experience with religion. Even though we may evoke a great deal of emotional transference with these people, they are confronted with a different model of religion when they see a pastor operating in a different setting.

One such person, a local businessman who had a negative impression of pastors, is now an active congregant who contributes a great deal of talent and support to our congregation. This relationship, which I now cherish, is a direct result of my community participation. Because of a friendship that had developed through a community project, I had been invited to a party by a local businesswoman who was involved in a congregation but whose husband was not. After the party she called me and said, "My husband wants to have lunch with you, because he doesn't believe you're a pastor." Apparently I had told some jokes and had been more of a real person than fitted his image of pastors. We had lunch and began a friendship that continues to grow. He later joined our congregation.

Though I'm not as overtly evangelistic as many others, I discovered what many already knew—when you show interest in someone, they show interest in you. When I became more interested in economic development, I got to know our county economic-development officer and learned that he was engaged to be married. He and his fiancée were active in different congregations, so they were looking for a new congregation where they could establish their family together. Because of our relationship with the community, they asked me to officiate at their wedding; later they joined our church. A similar thing happened when I became active in our chamber of commerce. As I got to know the chamber president, she told me that her family was looking for a church with a more active youth program. They soon visited our congregation and became active in several ministries. Later they moved their memberships to our church. Though these folks may have found our congregation on their own, I know that my involvement in community leadership had a direct bearing on their decision to join.

Even when a pastor's involvement in community leadership doesn't lead directly to the addition of new members, it can serve as a catalyst to church growth. For better or worse, every congregation develops a reputation within its community. We can either let the community develop its impression on its own—an impression that may or may not be accurate—or we can actively define ourselves. Although advertising and other techniques can be beneficial, the best outreach plan is always personal contact.

When our communities see pastors and other congregational leaders caring about issues beyond their congregation, they get a sense of a church that cares. When we remain isolated within our parish, people sense an inwardly focused organization that doesn't seem to care. Because my congregation has graciously shared its pastor within the community and because members themselves have gotten involved, our reputation has improved greatly. The evidence I have for this claim comes from community real estate agents, who tell me that they often list our congregation among others when clients ask about the best churches in town. Several people have visited our congregation because of a referral by their real estate agent, and some of them have joined. I've had the privilege of meeting many of these agents through community leadership. They often get involved in the community because they know that the health of the community has a direct impact on the strength of their business. I hope our congregations discover the same truth.

Your Choice

Despite my positive assessment of pastoral community leadership, some might wonder how those of us already loaded up with responsibilities can find the time and energy to take on community leadership as well. Others might wonder if they have the gifts and skills to expand their ministries into the larger community. As I stated earlier, community leadership is one possible piece of a ministry puzzle. It may or may not fit into your picture, but I hope you will at least pick it up, turn it around a few times, and see if it fits. Even if it doesn't meet a need in your ministry right now, perhaps it will later. When considering your response, however, remember that:

- There is a great need for community leadership.
- Our biblical predecessors provided leadership in their communities.
- Many of our congregational leadership skills translate well into community settings.
- There can be positive results for our congregations and ministries.

I have found community leadership both productive and enjoyable. But, as the stock market commercials say, "Results may vary." If you expand your ministry into community leadership, I hope your results are even better than mine.

Notes

Chapter 1, A Pastoral Response

1. Howard Clinebell, *Basic Types of Pastoral Care and Counseling* (Nashville: Abingdon, 1984), 107.
2. Ibid., 138.
3. Peter L. Steinke, *Healthy Congregations: A Systems Approach*, (Herndon, Va.: Alban Institute, 1996), 43.
4. Robert D. Putnam, "The Strange Disappearance of Civic America," *The American Prospect*, Dec. 1996 (accessed March 26, 2004, at www.prospect.org).
5. Ibid.
6. Project summary from forum "The Decline of Civic Involvement in America: Real or Imagined?" (Fort Lauderdale: Florida Atlantic University and Florida Institute of Government, April 25, 2002). The project summary is the result of a forum designed to inform and involve a group of citizens on the level of civic involvement in southeast Florida. More than 50 representatives from government agencies, nonprofit groups, charities, and other community-based organizations participated in the event.
7. Wade Clark Roof and William McKinney, *American Mainline Religion: Its Changing Shape and Future* (New Brunswick, N.J.: Rutgers University Press, 1987), 233.

8. Source: CNN/*USA Today*/Gallup Poll, Nov. 14-16, 2003, +/- 3 percent margin of error; sample size = 1,004 adults ages 18 and older. Web site: http://poll.gallup.com/ (accessed Sept. 1, 2004).

9. Ibid.

Chapter 2, Squirrels in the Road

1. I am thankful to my friend Ben Trawick, pastor of North Wilkesboro Presbyterian Church in North Wilkesboro, North Carolina, for suggesting the squirrel analogy.

2. Jim Kitchens, *The Postmodern Parish: New Ministry for a New Era* (Herndon, Va.: Alban Institute, 2003).

3. Brian D. McLaren, *The Church on the Other Side: Doing Ministry in the Postmodern Matrix* (Grand Rapids: Zondervan, 2000), 159.

4. See Wayne Gabardi, *Negotiating Postmodernism* (Minneapolis: University of Minnesota Press, 2001).

5. Zygmunt Bauman, *Life in Fragments: Essays in Postmodernism* (Oxford, U.K., and Cambridge, Mass.: Blackwell Publishers, 1995), 10.

6. McLaren, *Church on the Other Side*, 53.

7. H. Richard Niebuhr, *Christ and Culture* (New York: Harper & Row, 1951), 41.

8. Niebuhr also presents two other views: "Christ above culture," and "Christ and culture in paradox."

9. Gil Rendle, video "Living Into the New World: How Cultural Trends Affect Your Congregation" (Herndon, Va.: Alban Institute, 2000).

10. "Mayberry," performed by Rascal Flatts on CD "Melt," 2002.

11. John Pierce, *Baptists Today*, Atlanta, Ga., May, 2004.

12. Loren Mead, *The Once and Future Church* (Herndon, Va.: Alban Institute, 1991).
13. Stanley Hauerwas and William H. Willimon, *Resident Aliens* (Nashville: Abingdon, 1989), 18.

Chapter 3, Prophets, Priests, and Kings

1. Robert Cate, "Prophets," *The Mercer Dictionary of the Bible* (Macon, Ga.: Mercer University Press, 1990), 715.
2. Ibid.
3. D. Larry Gregg, "A Prophet's Royal Influence," *The Biblical Illustrator* (vol. 30, no. 4, summer 2004), 30.
4. Ibid., 28.
5. Ibid.
6. Jim Wallis, "Take Back the Faith," *Sojourners* (Sept. 2004, vol. 33, no. 9), 4.
7. Reidar B. Bjornard, "Priest," *The Mercer Dictionary of the Bible* (Macon, Ga.: Mercer Unviversity Press, 1990), 711.
8. Ibid., 710.
9. Bob Hulteen, "Once a Millennium," *Sojourners* (July-Aug. 1998, vol. 27, no. 4), 65.
10. Jim Wallis, "God's Politics: A Better Option," *Sojourners* (Feb. 2005, vol. 34, no. 2), 14.
11. Ibid.

Chapter 4, Community Needs

1. Tyson's mission statement is found at its Web site at www.tysonfoodsinc.com (accessed March 15, 2005).
2. Wayne Oates, *The Christian Pastor* (Philadelphia: Westminster Press, 1982), 128.

3. Adapted from Bruce Hamm, "What Is an Ethics Officer?" on "The CEO Refresher," Refresher Publications Inc., www.refresher.com/!bahofficer.html. (accessed April 4, 2005).
4. Burton H. Patterson, "Ethical Issues in Human Resource Management," *Christian Ethics Today* (Christmas 2004, vol. 10, no. 5), 18.
5. James M. Kouzes and Barry Z. Posner, "Leadership Is Everyone's Business," *Christian Reflections on the Leadership Challenge*, ed. James M. Kouzes and Barry Z. Posner (San Francisco: Jossey-Bass, 2004), 2.
6. Peter Steinke, *Healthy Congregations* (Herndon, Va.: Alban Institute, 1996), 35.

Chapter 5, Getting to It

1. Robert Putnam, *Bowling Alone: The Collapse and Revival of American Community* (New York: Simon & Schuster, 2000), 66.
2. Ibid., 401.
3. Ibid.
4. For more information see Edward H. Hammett's article "Keeping People over Sixty While Reaching People under Forty," May/June, 2003 issue of *Net Results* magazine. Or you may order it in the *Involving More Young Adults (Gens X & Y)* reprint pack available at www.netresults.org.

Chapter 6, Moving Outside Our Comfort Zone

1. For more information see Duke Divinity School's Web site, *Divinity Online* (winter 2004, volume 3, no. 2) at http://

www.divinity.duke.edu/publications/2004.01/features/
neighborhood/print.htm (accessed June 19, 2005).

2. The pamphlet *Religion in the Public Schools: A Joint Statement of Law*, produced by over 40 groups as diverse as the American Jewish Committee, the National Council of Churches, the National Sikh Center, and various Christian groups, is an excellent resource for pastors and educators. It is available from a number of religious and secular sources, including the Baptist Joint Committee at (202) 544-4226. The BJC Web site is www.bjcpa.org.

3. Putnam, *Bowling Alone,* 66.

4. Ibid., 78-79.

5. Len Eberhart, "Closing Rural Congregations," in *Ending with Hope: A Resource for Closing Congregations*, Beth Ann Gaede, ed. (Herndon, Va.: Alban Institute, 2002), 101.

6. Jeffrey Brown, "Turning Tragedy Into Triumph," *Sojourners,* (March-April 1998, vol. 27, no. 2), 13.

7. Taken from the Boston Ten Point Coalition Web site: bostontenpt.users2.50megs.com/index.html (accessed June 18, 2005).

8. For more information on the Christian Women's Job Corps, visit its Web site at www.wmu.com/getinvolved/ministry/cwjc/.

9. Putnam, *Bowling Alone,* 402-403.